Praise for *Layered Leadership*

"*Layered Leadership* by Lawrence Armstrong is a master class in growth. Growing annual revenues? Yes. Growing one's skill set from managing a paper route to owning and leading a company with $100 million a year in revenues and offices across the world? Yes. Growing one's ability to manage and, more importantly, lead people? Yes. Growing in wealth, authority, power, prestige, and success while remaining humble and focused on your people and their needs? Yes. Growing through hard work, putting in the hours, and yet also taking care of the body, mind, and soul through play and unstructured time off? Yes. On each and every page of his valuable book, Armstrong layers authenticity on top of humility, ability, and success to build an imminently useful how-to manual for work and life."

—Todd Diacon, President, Kent State University

"Lawrence Armstrong's *Layered Leadership* captures the key to building successful organizations by developing well-rounded leaders. I've personally watched and admired Larry's impressive journey from our first project in 1986 to now. This book shares valuable strategies for encouraging creativity and driving steady growth, no matter the economic climate. This book proves the power of strategic mentorship and visionary leadership. Larry's dual passions for business and art shine through, offering a fresh perspective on leadership that's both practical and inspirational."

—Ted Antenucci, President & CEO,
Catellus Development Corporation

"This book is a must read for anyone striving to build a successful business and, most importantly, a successful life. His insight into how you bring your whole self into any endeavor is inspiring. In every encounter with Larry, you leave energized and committed to do more. Rarely does one meet such an accomplished and respected leader. In *Layered Leadership*, we all now have the opportunity to learn how to infuse creativity, discipline, humanity, and passion into everything we do...including addressing complex societal issues such as homelessness. Thank you, Larry!"

—Susan B. Parks, President & CEO, OC United Way

"*Layered Leadership* is a transformative guide for modern leaders seeking to inspire and drive real change. Larry's extensive experience in guiding high-performing teams shines through in this book, offering actionable

insights and strategies that blend visionary thinking with practical application. This book is essential for executives and managers aiming to build resilient, innovative teams and achieve sustained success. Larry's dual expertise in business and art adds a unique, creative dimension to his pragmatic strategies, making this a must-read for anyone seeking to elevate their leadership game."
—Lew Horne, President, Advisory Services CBRE, GLA-OC-IE

"*Layered Leadership* dives into how investing in people can lead to organizational greatness. Through Ware Malcomb's rise to industry leadership, Larry emphasizes the importance of developing well-rounded leaders and fostering a culture of innovation and mentorship. This book is a must-have for leaders focused on sustainable growth and building a lasting legacy of excellence. Larry's experience as an artist enriches his approach to leadership, blending creativity with strategic foresight."
—Dick Gochnauer, Former CEO, Essendant

"I thoroughly enjoyed *Layered Leadership*, a must-read for anyone interested in the intersection of art, architecture, and business. It is not just about leadership but about building and sustaining a successful business. I particularly enjoyed his references to *Good to Great*, my favorite management book. That said, let's appreciate that this was not written by some consultant or business pundit but by someone with personal insights who has "walked the talk"! Lastly, Lawrence's writing style, and his own artwork included with each chapter, make this an enjoyable page-turner."
—Steve Swerdlow, Principal, Swerdlow Advisory
and Former Group President, CBRE

Layered Leadership

Layered Leadership

Drive Double-Digit Growth and Dominate Your Competition with Creative Strategies and Execution

Lawrence R. Armstrong

Matt Holt Books
An Imprint of BenBella Books, Inc.
Dallas, TX

Layered Leadership copyright © 2025 by Layered Vision, LLC

Matt Holt is an imprint of BenBella Books, Inc.
8080 N. Central Expressway
Suite 1700
Dallas, TX 75206
benbellabooks.com
Send feedback to feedback@benbellabooks.com

BenBella and *Matt Holt* are federally registered trademarks.

Printed in the United States of America
10 9 8 7 6 5 4 3 2 1

Library of Congress Control Number: 2024034198
ISBN 9781637746356 (hardcover)
ISBN 9781637746363 (electronic)

Editing by Lydia Choi
Copyediting by Michael Fedison
Proofreading by Sarah Vostok and Cape Cod Compositors, Inc.
Text design and composition by PerfecType, Nashville, TN
Cover design by Lawrence R. Armstrong and Monica Birakos
Graphic images by Lawrence R. Armstrong, Noah Burrows, and Monica Birakos
Images on on pages 56 and 205 were generated with Bing AI Image, powered by Dall-E
Printed by Sheridan MI

This book is dedicated to all the people who have helped and inspired me, and all of the people I hope to help and inspire.

CONTENTS

AUTHOR'S NOTE

I was given an incredible opportunity to lead our company. Along the way, I've discovered my own way to bring creativity to leadership— by synthesizing influences, metaphors, and life lessons into a style of leadership that helps people gain a different perspective and insight into leading and motivating people and building a company. Over time, I've been asked by many people to share how we have built our company and if I would advise or mentor someone to help build theirs.

That's why I wrote this book.

Part One

The Foundation– Staying Balanced

Introduction: Flashes of Light

I grew up a block from the Grand River, which winds its way through my hometown of Painesville, Ohio, to Lake Erie. When I was born, we lived in a small ranch house on a street of ranch houses. We were a half-hour drive to Cleveland and a Saturday morning drive to Headlands Beach State Park on the Lake. Dad was an industrial chemist and Mom a homemaker.

Nelmar Drive is a straight residential street, framing the front lawns of our homes, ending in the river's elevated green bank. My brothers and I rode our bikes and played sandlot sports with tons of neighborhood kids on that quiet street. All the kids made it less quiet and very active.

When I was in first grade, our parents decided our house was too small. Dad bought the vacant lot next door and hired a builder to construct our family a new house—from the ground up.

On weekends, our family piled in the family station wagon to drive around Northeast Ohio, checking out different new homes that builders were offering. My parents hired one they liked, and by the time I was in second grade, our family was watching our new home go up on the newly graded lot. I'd come home after school and wander around the jobsite after the workers left. Probably not an activity parents would allow these days, but these were the mid-1960s, and kids in a town like ours had a lot of freedom as long as they were home by dinnertime. Parents didn't hover the way they do now.

From when our house was just a hole in the ground to the time the framing went up and the house was built, I found various vantage points of exploration, fascinated by the white two-story Colonial. I watched all the stages of construction, curious about the wood frame, the windows, the way open spaces became rooms where my family would live. I was eight years old.

When you are a kid and a sponge for whatever the world lights up for you, and the spotlight is on buildings, you see how all buildings contain layers. Our house did, and so do human dwellings through-

out history. The ox bones, felt, and skins of the Mongolian tent. The aspen poles, buffalo blankets, and exterior skins of the teepee. Then there is the clay and straw of African huts, or the Irish country cottage of the 19th century made with local stones and clay, covered with a thatch roof stuffed with bog turf.

Since the new house was next door, we moved in over a few days. I still remember that first night, surrounded by my

FLR 1.15 MOV (36" x 48"). Mixed media on board.

brothers' excitement, the new space, color, and smell of new carpet, my own room with a view from the second floor. I spent my childhood and teenage years there and was always building things from erector sets to Tinkertoys to tree houses. The project deeply inspired me.

Not long after the house was completed, I discovered a new indoor shopping mall had started construction downtown. I hopped on my bike and rode off to this mysterious excavation of much greater scale than our home project on Nelmar Drive. In the months ahead, I climbed all over that construction site (after hours) to see the construction progress: the materials, the steel frame, the bundled yellow lumber stacked, hoisted, and nailed to the sky. Finally, there was brick and mortar's patient artistry followed by panes of glass put into place. I was compelled by the process, how different materials came together and in what sequence, and the tools used to achieve the result.

Then, one 10th-grade summer, I had a job at the local library and used the reference books to research college architecture programs. I found about four, five, or six I wanted to apply to, and Kent State University was one of them. My dad and I visited several of the universities, but for me, Kent State stood out from the others. I loved the beautiful campus and how well rounded the program was. It wasn't focused only on one thing. It was focused on the whole thing.

Not only did I get my architecture degree at Kent State, but during my fourth year in a five-year program, I had the chance to study abroad in Florence, an experience transformative to my perspective and ways of thinking. When you're a middle-class kid from the Midwest and get an opportunity to travel to a European country, it just changes your whole life. Leonardo da Vinci became my greatest professor (more on him later).

I met Sandy in high school. She ended up sitting right in front of me in our American Government class senior year. I liked her—she was super cute and interesting—so I made it my mission to get to know her a little bit in class and worked up the nerve to ask her out after a couple of months. I remember dialing those numbers on the rotary phone the first time I called. I was pretty nervous. She said yes, and we never looked back.

When I went to Kent, she attended a community college in our town. Then the next year, she came down to Kent State as a transfer student. We got married in Kent right after I graduated in 1980. Sandy is my most trusted advisor and a creative and effective leader as cochair with me on the Kent State Campaign Executive Committee.

"Layers of space define the project and begin to emanate from the hills, valley, and ocean on our horizons."

We were very fortunate to be able to design and build our own home, a dream for many architects. Achieving this dream brought me full circle from the home my parents built for our own family.

"Our house was always your laboratory of layers," Sandy once said to me. "It is such a great example in terms of architecture."

The house we designed is a complex structure, pure white, nestled in green surroundings. Fundamental to understanding this building is the concept of layers; correspondingly, the building is a perfect visual exploration of this idea. The plan derives from two shifted grids, aligned with different geometries of the property and bordering streets. The external layer, itself constructed of many smaller layers, wraps around the architectural skeleton of the building and creates almost infinitely complex divisions of three-dimensional volume.

Layers of space define the project and begin to emanate from the hills, valley, and ocean on our horizons. Outdoor spaces, site walls, and landscape elements provide organized layers leading to the exterior façade. The exterior wall is itself a study in layers, a solid void composition of plaster, metal, and glass. The exposed structural columns and brise-soleil* provide another spatial layer, and as you experience space deeper into the house, layers manifest in solid and

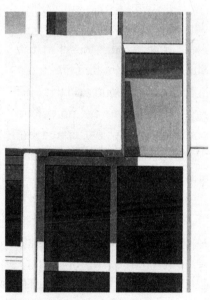

Figure 1. Layers generate intrigues of space.

---

* An architectural feature of a building that reduces heat gain within that building by deflecting sunlight.

glass walls, railings, and elements defining the public and private zones. (See figure 1.)

Plaster panels form the exterior walls. Glazing elements form a transparent layer, a view into the interior of the building, and the layers of space beyond the perimeter.

The way I conceive my art, the way I provide leadership, and the way I built my company is in layers.

For designers and architects, we always deal in three-dimensional layers of space. But layers aren't only found in our built environment. Layers occur in the natural world and the built world. They can be perceived not only in physical space but also in atmospheric, intellectual, and emotional space.

Layers of topography around the Provo River. By the riverbank, an angler chooses a trout fly.

"To seek the timeless way, we must first know the quality without a name," wrote the late and legendary architect and urbanist Christopher Alexander. "There is a central quality which is the root criterion of life and spirit in a man, a town, a building, or a wilderness."

He wrote, "Intuitively we may guess that the beauty of a building, its life, and its capacity to support life all come from the fact that it is working as a whole. A view of the building as a whole means that we see it as part of an extended and undivided continuum. It is not an isolated fragment in itself, but part of the world which includes the gardens, walls, trees, streets beyond its boundaries, and other buildings beyond those."[1]

> "Intuitively we may guess that the beauty of a building, its life, and its capacity to support life all come from the fact that it is working as a whole. A view of the building as a whole means that we see it as part of an extended and undivided continuum. It is not an isolated fragment in itself, but part of the world which includes the gardens, walls, trees, streets beyond its boundaries, and other buildings beyond those."
>
> —Christopher Alexander

The natural environment undulates and changes as layers shift from plains to tree lines to mountains to riverbanks and the layers of current in the river itself. Geological wonders such as the Middle Provo River in Utah, where I love to go fly-fishing, exemplify the visual and living layers of our earth. The lush grasslands of the valley gradate in rolling curves, becoming forested ridges and then giving way to the slabs of granitic and volcanic layers of the Wasatch Range. We are highly conscious of boundaries in how we see, navigate, and explore nature.

Physical layers are one aspect of how you experience the world. Another way is with light. If I am in my office at Ware Malcomb, natural light enters the space from the exterior. There are shadows that it creates. There's an LED light from above my head. On my desk, light glows from the computer screen.

> **Physical layers are one aspect of how you experience the world. Another way is with light.**

Sound surrounds us in layers. In my office, I hear one seam of voices outside the door; another is the hum of the air-conditioning duct above; yet another is the barely audible traffic noise from the adjacent street. Music is filled with layers, integrated layers, of instruments, sound effects, and vocals. Musical tracks are produced in separate instrumental and vocal layers and then integrated and synthesized. I like to focus on one particular instrument when I'm listening and then perceive all of the other layers around it in the song.

As the reader, you experience layers as you read a book: the first layer is processing the words as they appear on the page, but you also experience different emotions and thoughts as you read, and your senses pick up on different inputs around you, some of which you notice and some you do not.

Layering Leadership Lessons

What does all this have to do with you? Leadership, whether of a start-up; small, mid-sized, or large firm; team; church; or any organization, must work as a whole across the continuum of functions and people, comprised of many layers, but not in the traditional manner of layers of management in a bureaucratic org chart. We are discussing a more conceptual way of perceiving and synthesizing layers of disparate influences, methodologies, and learning.

The leadership processes and operational strategies that I have learned over time will lead to better outcomes and more goals achieved for any manager or leader in any profession or industry who reads these pages, does the explorations, and implements changes as they fit your particular situation. Layers are a metaphor, a methodology, and a framework for synthesizing the vast amount of knowledge required for our lives and work.

> **Layers are a metaphor, a methodology, and a framework for synthesizing the vast amount of knowledge required for our lives and work.**

I believe that by adopting these strategies, you will see more positive outcomes and faster business and personal growth than you've known.

Integral to what I teach and share is that this kind of leadership is creative. It's about synthesizing input from many varied sources. It's about bringing your whole self to the team and the objective. No layer in life is constrained by another layer. Just as a painting transcends the frame (see figure 2), leaders can transcend job description (and not to *do* more but *make more* of what they do).

Figure 2. *Gestalt.* Layered metal. The art transcends the frame.

My inspiration for art, business, leadership, and even parenting comes from many different places. Sometimes it's a word said in passing, sometimes a painting, sometimes a play of light and shadow on a tree, sometimes a sunrise, sometimes a song that's on the radio. Our studies of other companies outside our industry led to creative applications at Ware Malcomb. I've experienced breakthrough insights for my art and our company in nature, listening to music, taking a walk.

I refer to these revelations as flashes of light.

I will demonstrate techniques and methods for nurturing breakthrough creative thinking and idea formation in this book. I encourage you to challenge yourself with this approach. Many people don't think of themselves as creative. I believe everyone is creative.

Back on Nelmar Drive at the Armstrong house construction site, a flash of light arrived one summer afternoon: when I grew up, I wanted to be involved with the building process. I followed that realization through my decision to study architecture at Kent State. Years later, while guiding our business to national prominence, several more flashes of light illuminated critical strategic directions.

If you're reading this book, you know what it means to make a difference with your team, company, profession, faith, and family. You know what it means to see and grab hold of critical opportunities. Now that you know a bit about me, in the next chapter we'll turn to how this book will help you learn and do more consistently as a leader, day to day.

I'm an optimist (my grandmother taught me to be one). I try to practice gratitude for all I have every day. I tried to demonstrate this in my writing when our Vistage group was challenged to write a poem on the spot in one of our meetings.

Soon after, I was given the honor to deliver a commencement address at Kent State University, and I incorporated that poem into my remarks:

Time

The light of daybreak brings a gift
To be cared for
To not relinquish to idleness
To be rejoiced in
To not be squandered

The fall of darkness brings a gift
To feel accomplished
To not relinquish to disappointment
To cherish
To not despair

How to Use This Book

"Commitment is what transforms a promise into reality."

—Abraham Lincoln

Going to California

The next layer of my life's journey from Painesville to this book started to emerge when Sandy moved to Kent State in my sophomore year. We were happy together during college and were married shortly after I graduated in 1980.

I secured my first job out of school in a town neighboring Kent State while Sandy was finishing her degree. It was a small firm, and they paid me five dollars an hour. That's a dollar per hour for every year I went to school . . . awesome! It was 1981, and my first job as an architect lasted only eight months.

The United States experienced the worst recession since the Great Depression, which had a particularly devastating impact on construction and manufacturing in the Rust Belt. This downturn was later surpassed by the 2007–2008 financial crisis. "The nearly 11 percent unemployment rate reached late in 1982 remains the apex of the post World War II era (Federal Reserve Bank of St. Louis)," noted Tim Sablik of the Federal Reserve in a history of the period.[2] "Unemployment during the 1981–82 recession was widespread, but manufacturing, construction, and the auto industries were particularly affected. Although goods producers accounted for only 30 percent of total employment at the time, they suffered 90 percent of job losses in 1982. Three fourths of all job losses in the goods-producing sector were in manufacturing, and the residential construction industry and auto manufacturers ended the year with 22 percent and 24 percent unemployment, respectively."[3]

Aiming to fight inflation, the Reagan administration and Fed chair Paul Volcker tightened the money supply, which raised interest rates and, therefore, the cost of borrowing.

The economy was suffering, and so were millions of people. It was a grim time to live around Cleveland; so many companies slowing down and laying off people. By 1982, Ohio's 12.5 percent was the second-highest unemployment figure of any state.

So, early in 1981, my boss called me into his office and told me he couldn't support the staff anymore. There were five of us, and he let the two most junior people go. It was rough; Sandy and I didn't know what to do. We didn't have a nest egg or safety net. I had to find another job, but it felt like it would be a long time until I did.

A number of my college friends had moved to Southern California after graduating. The night before they pulled out of Ohio for points west, we had a couple beers to say goodbye and wish them luck.

I had never considered leaving. I loved Ohio, I still do, and thought I would build my career in Cleveland. I started talking to my friends on the West Coast, and they urged us to consider going out there, insisting that there were lots of jobs. I called my dad to ask for his advice. He said, "You don't have kids yet, you don't have a house yet—there's nothing holding you here. If you want to try a move like this, now's the time." It was Sandy who made the final decision. She said, "You know what? We should do this. We should go."

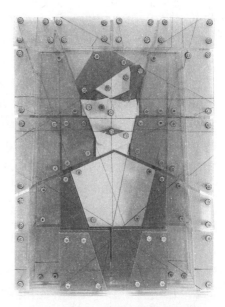

Amor 1.1 **(12" x 15" x 8"). Layered painted glass and stainless steel.**

I got a temporary job at an architectural firm in Canton. I was lucky to get the job, and they were up front in telling me it was temporary and that they couldn't guarantee how long it would last. We saved up as much money as we could in a couple of months, about five hundred bucks. We packed our life up into an old Cutlass my parents had given to me. It was in good working condition, and we made it across the country in five nights, staying in motels along the way.

We started by crashing on the floor in my friend Geoff Lester's studio apartment in Santa Ana. For two weeks, our bed was on the floor in sleeping bags, and we went out looking for jobs. Our tiny nest egg was running out.

Luckily, we both secured jobs. Sandy worked in a real estate office, and I was fortunate to be hired at an architectural firm. We found a small one-bedroom apartment. There was a Sears wholesale store down the street. We bought a mattress (not a bed) and threw it on the floor. It felt like the start of our lives together.

It was a big risk to move across the country like that. Finding the leader within you at some point requires betting on yourself and your abilities. You have to know when to take that risk and why you are doing it. That the economy had cratered in Ohio made the risk more manageable, but still, we were leaving what we knew, where we had our families and many friends. When you dive off the high board, it's scary. But we had each other and naïve confidence.

> It was a big risk to move across the country like that. Finding the leader within you at some point requires betting on yourself and your abilities. You have to know when to take that risk and why you are doing it. That the economy had cratered in Ohio made the risk more manageable, but still, we were leaving what we knew, where we had our families and many friends.

I ended up working at a thriving family-run firm for about three years and secured my architectural license. I learned a lot, but it was a small firm without much room for growth, so I decided to move on. After sending out a small number of resumes, I got a call about a week later from Bill Malcomb, cofounder along with Bill Ware of Ware Malcomb Architects. He invited me to come in for an interview, and the firm ended up hiring me.

In a year and a half, I went from designer to project manager; then, Bill and Bill offered me a new post to open and run an office in

Woodland Hills in the San Fernando Valley in Los Angeles. It was an amazing opportunity to learn many things about leadership. The San Fernando office faced intense competition, and we had to learn how to understand our competition and their strengths and weaknesses; we had to position ourselves in the best way relative to them. Eventually, our office became the most profitable one in the company.

I'll pick up on my story in the next chapter on skills development.

Firm cofounders Bill Ware and Bill Malcomb.

What You Will Learn in This Book

In 2023, *Building Design + Construction* magazine (the platinum standard publication for our industry) named Ware Malcomb the number one industrial architecture and engineering firm in America for the third year in a row.[4]

Reaching that kind of success is about developing leaders. I knew it when I was promoted, and my life has proven it a hundredfold in the decades that followed. That's why I wrote this book. My goal is to bring to as many readers as possible the successes of supporting and mentoring team members that are instrumental to Ware Malcomb's leadership academy and similar practices in other great companies.

> **My goal is to bring to as many readers as possible the successes of supporting and mentoring team members that are instrumental to Ware Malcomb's leadership academy and similar practices in other great companies. Developing leaders is one of my life's most powerful and impactful discoveries and satisfactions.**

Developing leaders is one of my most powerful and impactful discoveries and satisfactions. I've been a student of other leaders throughout my life and enormously lucky to have had great leaders show me what matters. When Jim Williams and I took over the company as president and CEO, respectively, our firm was a great regional Southern California architectural firm, and we weren't sure how to grow. We tried hiring senior managers based on their resumes, reputations, and recommendations. Some of them worked out; many didn't. We were watching an escalator of folks riding into the firm and exiting soon after when they didn't fit. Jim related it to the experience of President Lincoln. When Lincoln was fighting the Civil War, he had to keep firing his top generals because they were too cautious, avoiding failure and not seeking victory. Finally losing his patience, Lincoln was famously quoted as saying, "If General McClellan does not want to use the army, I would like to borrow it for a time." After demoting seven generals, Lincoln promoted Ulysses S. Grant, and he won the war.

We realized that experiencing and developing within our culture was the missing ingredient. We had some key young people rising within our ranks, including our current CEO, Kenneth Wink. We hired Ken as a new project manager, and we immediately noticed that, in addition to his excellent abilities as an architect, he possessed a leadership ability and a robust set of skills in working with people. We asked him to take on a new leadership assignment. All we did was mention it. Next thing we knew, he was holding a meeting in the back of the office, putting it all together with the right people and getting it done—exactly what we had asked him to do. I told Jim, "Look what can happen with empowerment and opportunity."

Having witnessed the power of this example, we decided to emphasize, promote, and refine these values throughout our culture. We love it when people come into Ware Malcomb, understand our culture, learn what we are trying to do, believe in it, and embrace it. We love giving people opportunities. It's so important to me that we give people chances to grow when they are committed to our company; that is what happened to me.

I was fortunate to be chosen to, first of all, run an office; then, second of all, have the opportunity to buy the company. At the time, I knew I wanted to take this company as far as I possibly could, and I wanted to give as many people opportunities to grow as possible. For us, this idea fueled our success. We have grown exponentially, but not primarily by acquiring other firms. We make the occasional acquisition but mostly hire people. We hire a lot of people. Our preferred method is to grow organically, establish new offices, and promote people from within to run those offices. We have numerous team members who have been with us for many years because they have been able to respond to an opportunity and take a risk. It's a great way to build a company. When you acquire a smaller firm or bring in a senior person from outside, you need time for people to acclimate to your culture.

Bringing your whole self to work, cultivating your diverse capabilities, and identifying the best career opportunities is an excellent way for you to develop as a leader. It's a great way to build a culture. The book is designed to help you do that.

The book contains three primary layers:

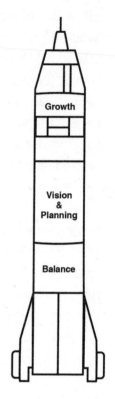

- **Part One: The Foundation—Staying Balanced**
- **Part Two: Develop a Vision, Build a Plan**
- **Part Three: Strategic Growth**

Each piece is similar in scope and length, building upon the last. First, you need a good foundation individually as a leader. Second, you need to sharpen and build out your vision and plan. Then you'll be prepared to lead your business toward purposeful growth and gain market share from your competitors.

Part One: The Foundation—Staying Balanced

The art of leadership begins with the search for knowledge and self-awareness. We'll use Leonardo da Vinci as a model for learning whole-brain thinking. Leonardo was not only an artist but someone with diverse life experiences and a huge range in his skill set. He didn't just build on his strengths. He had technical and theoretical training and interpersonal skills that helped him network and connect with influential people, a profound curiosity, and many interests in different subjects. I consider Leonardo to be the greatest genius the world has ever known.

We'll use Leonardo da Vinci as a model for learning whole-brain thinking. Leonardo was not only an artist but someone with diverse life experiences and a huge range in his skill set. He didn't just build on his strengths. He had technical and theoretical training and interpersonal skills that helped him network and connect with influential people, a profound curiosity, and many interests in different subjects.

Being a whole-brain leader involves layers of skills: formal (education), leadership, interpersonal, and creative skills.

We'll walk through a series of questions regarding your current skills portfolio; based on your responses, I'll assign you homework. Your first Exploration Sketchbook assignment will be an end-of-day creative exercise.

In chapter 2, we will focus on the importance of being aware of others. This includes understanding people with different backgrounds from your own, striking a balance between listening and advocating, and recognizing the creativity that everyone brings to the table. We will cover useful strategies such as coaching, the Chessboard approach, and always having a trusted second in command. These skills are critical for leadership development.

I'll also discuss what I learned working on the homelessness issue in Orange County, California, and how critical it is to open our external focus to those around us who need help.

In chapter 3, we shift our attention toward leadership, and we will learn to incorporate skills such as active listening and unlocking creativity in all aspects of our lives. You will discover how to strengthen your leadership awareness by teaming up for generative innovation and partnering on a creative challenge, a formal mentoring ethos, and the cornerstones of mentoring. The chapter details the significance of effective leadership meetings and how to build a strategic plan. Additionally, we will learn about the role of an indispensable Number Two and the importance of promoting your best people.

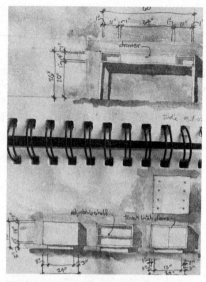

Chapter 4 is my personal health manifesto: showing you the benefits of layered habits to achieve balance physically and mentally. Establish a base layer of wellness upon which you layer other habits. These vary depending on your interests and fitness.

Images from my sketchbook.

The Chinese martial art of tai chi, which concentrates on balance, strength, flexibility, and inner calm, is one example. Good sleep always, meditation, and eating healthy are others. I love skiing, and while that is a seasonal sport, it inspires me to stay fit year-round. I've made a concerted effort not to be a workaholic in my life, and delegation skills are essential.

Part Two: Develop a Vision, Build a Plan

When you are the leader, when you are the CEO, leading a business unit or a small business, your thought process must be out in front of your company. Think about where the company is going, where you want it to go, and how you are going to always get there. You need to look into the future. Commit your vision to paper, not just in your mind but also by mapping out where your company's potential can be achieved. This changes everything.

When you take the time and energy to lay out your vision, it gives you a basis of what to do every day, every year, every five years to achieve that goal. When you are writing your business plan for the upcoming year, you can view that as a step toward your long-term vision. Each year's plan represents an opportunity to build toward your ultimate vision.

> When you are the leader, when you are the CEO, leading a business unit or a small business, your thought process needs to be out in front of your company. You need to be thinking about where the company is going, where you want it to go, and how you are going to always get there. You need to look into the future.

This is the strategy by which we've designed our company. It involves the use of specific business plans that are created each year and then repeatedly tested to ensure they align with our mission, incentivize innovation, include succession planning, prepare us for economic shocks, and promote the development of strong leaders. Most important, even with all of these factors in place, is to build a strong company culture.

Authors and consultants have published bewildering stacks of studies and books on strategic planning. They can leave you over-whelmed with lingo. Chapter 5 provides you with a jargon-free process to simplify and stress test a one-page actionable plan for your business or unit or team. I'll discuss research methods for identifying pathways to success depending on your organization and sector. One tool is de-layering similar businesses to understand what led to success or failure, such as Home Depot versus the failed HomeClub, which were founded within five years of each other with similar business goals.

I'll share how we adopted W. Chan Kim and Renée Maurborgne's method for identifying "blue ocean" layers in your industry or vertical for expansion.[5] We don't want to swim in a red ocean. We want to swim in a blue ocean. (Red oceans are crowded with businesses that are fighting for a share of the market, while blue oceans represent new and uncharted territories with potential for growth and innovation.) One way we do that is by looking at examples—such as Yellow Tail wines, which found a blue ocean in an industry choked with competitors, an industry where a lot of people lose a lot of money.

Chapter 6 is where I run a master strategy class in setting double-digit growth goals and then beating them.

At Ware Malcomb, we work as One Team across the United States and the Americas. A unified culture that rewards teamwork and mentoring and does not tolerate gossip or infighting takes meticulous planning, design, and training. That aspect of leadership is the focus of chapter 7.

In chapter 8, "The Visible Light Spectrum," you'll get a process for calibrating with accuracy the type and scale of diversification. At Ware Malcomb, we specialize in commercial real estate: the basis for our firm is designing industrial and office buildings for speculative commercial developers. We were and are a commercial real estate–focused design firm. It was our specialty at our founding and still is. We understand our clients' businesses. We understand what is going to make them successful and design great architecture that stands the test of time and holds long-term real estate value. To serve your clients, it's important to understand what makes them successful.

We also learned how the commercial real estate industry is vulnerable to the ups and downs of the economy. When the economy goes down, nobody is building anything speculative.

In our business, we know when a recession is looming because the phones stop ringing. When the early '90s recession threatened Ware Malcomb, we set out to diversify our company carefully and strategically.

Many design firms make the mistake of announcing, "We do everything." We didn't do that, and neither should you. We decided to compete in sectors that are closely aligned to our core business but provided a buffer against recessions. We would go into areas where we could lead and dominate our market share, a productive strategy since the mid-'90s.

At that time, we developed our metaphor of the Visible Light Spectrum for diversification, as seen in figure 1, which we'll expand on later. We've tested and retested our portfolio strategy on the Visible Light Spectrum, and the result has been fast, purposeful growth to national leadership. We've implemented the approach at companies we've acquired and advised: the results have rocked.

This chapter will teach the process for focusing on what you're great at.

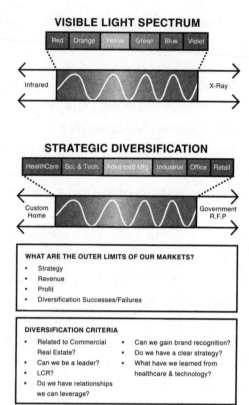

Figure 1. Workshopping the Visible Light Spectrum.

At this point, you'll have a strategic focus for competitive advantage. You'll have a plan for your team, your company, your consultant firm, your nonprofit, your franchise chain. Whatever the enterprise, leaders can have a detailed vision of mission and objectives but still fail to communicate through their workforce the direction or the culture required for success. The timeless Peter Drucker, one of the most influential management thinkers in history, wrote that leaders must embrace "the task of building and leading organizations in which every person sees herself as a 'manager' and accepts the full burden of what is basically managerial responsibility: responsibility for her own job and work group [and] for her contribution to the performance and results of the entire organization."[6]

Manage things, Drucker said, but lead people. He often used the parable of the three stonecutters: While walking, a traveler came across three stonecutters and asked each of them what they were doing. The first replied, "I am making a living." The second kept on hammering and replied, "I am doing the best job of stone cutting in the entire county." The third stopped, looked up at the traveler with a visionary gleam in his eye, and said, "I am building a cathedral."

Chapter 9, "Making Innovation Work," provides a step-by-step guide on how to create a culture of innovation within an organization. The chapter highlights the importance of innovation in an organization's strategic planning and goals and emphasizes that it should not be limited to a designated R&D unit but instead become an important aspect of corporate culture.

I explain how to develop a positive, uplifting culture for individuals and teams by drawing inspiration from our company's history and providing detailed guidance on how to integrate innovation into the organization's practices and operations.

This chapter provides studies of how we understand our clients' businesses and work innovatively to provide solutions to help them be successful, such as designing:

- Mid-rise office buildings using less expensive structural steel frames than competing buildings, along with more cost-effective use of exterior skin materials. Lower cost, lower rent, faster occupancy, faster cash flow.

- Articulated tilt-up panels to incorporate into a low-rise office headquarters. Lower cost, more attractive design, faster construction, faster occupancy, faster cash flow.

- Campuses of small office buildings for sale using lower-cost building materials (concrete block) with higher-quality finish. Lower cost, faster construction, faster sales, faster cash flow.

Numerous consultants and gurus herald creativity, the cognitive event of original ideas, in our culture and leadership. We know from neuroscience that when the individual has an original idea—when the proverbial light bulb goes on—it is exciting and motivating. Certainly, we have all been in situations or businesses where the way our boss acts or the business is run dampens, or kills, those creative impulses. As with instilling cultural practices in a business, creativity matters to those early layers of leadership. This book will nourish your spirit of creativity and infuse this energy into the layers of your company's development.

Many of us don't think of ourselves as creative. My experience and hard-won view is that everyone is creative if they adopt a continuous-learning, whole-brain approach. Whether that describes you or not, we all have strengths and weaknesses. As opposed to feeling bad about your weaknesses or areas of inexperience, Vince Lombardi said, view those as windows into where you are in your life and your career. It is your responsibility to accept that information about yourself, to do better, to take it further, to take your growth as far as you possibly can. Make the decision that today is a day when you decide to strengthen your game. Every day, train and improve, take another step—and soon those steps will become giant ones.

Many of us don't think of ourselves as creative. My experience and hard-won view is that everyone is creative if they adopt a continuous-learning, whole-brain approach. Whether that describes you or not, we all have strengths and weaknesses. As opposed to feeling bad about your weaknesses or areas of inexperience, Vince Lombardi said, view those as windows into where you are in your life and your career.

Part Three: Strategic Growth

Do you want to know what it takes to beat the competition and how to layer a successful acquisition, grow a unit within a business to become indispensable, and manage business development, operations, and sales to stay nimble as you grow? We offer an advanced course on growth and market leadership that we embellish with stories, metaphors, and illustrations, such as the Road Runner and the Coyote.

In chapter 10, "Embracing Your Hedgehog," I'll illustrate how to master this transition and have your Hedgehog serve as the basis for strategic growth. The Hedgehog is all of us putting in the work, the grind of building a company, and doing the hard things for many years. Then, suddenly, as Jim Collins explains, the Flywheel kicks in. This is exactly what happened to us, and it is why we doubled in revenue during the COVID-19 pandemic. Discipline and diligence are required for this to work.

Some leaders and, without question, some competitors of Ware Malcomb are afraid to embrace the idea of empowerment and building up your people. But it's necessary to build the temperament to hire supersmart people and then empower and guide them. By doing so, you tap into more talent, more energy, and more aspirational drive to achieve the company's, unit's, or team's mission. Fostering a culture that stays nimble as you grow encourages your leaders to move together in formation. An ocean liner takes time to maneuver into a new direction, and certainly there are giants in every industry that operate in this manner. On the other hand, a fleet of ships moves in the same direction but can change course faster without losing speed.

Nimble growth comes into sharper focus in chapter 11, which addresses how you can layer strategies for business expansion and growth. In the early days of my career at Ware Malcomb, Bill and Bill had the opportunity to open additional offices for the company, which has been headquartered in Irvine throughout its history. We established offices in San Diego and the San Fernando Valley, which Jim and I were fortunate to run. The success of these two operations formed the basis of establishing the company's culture of building effective and successful regional offices.

After Jim and I took over the company's leadership, some of our clients (Catellus, the Koll Company) requested our services in Northern California and Denver, Colorado, which led to the establishment of our first out-of-state office. We then identified critical markets across the United States and North America where our clients had a significant presence and developed a strategy to establish offices in all of those locations. As opportunities arose, we pursued this idea and developed a proactive growth strategy that we still implement today, which I will lay out in detail.

A few years ago, during the company's 50th anniversary, I was asked what advice I would give a new leader. I said it's vital not to take yourself too seriously and to continue to learn and aim to become a lifelong learner. I have a passion for continuous improvement, and I bet you do as well. I've discussed the concept with many leaders over the years that it's critical to understand every area of your business. Being well rounded enables you to manage a developing business and fill in any gaps. It is equally critical for success to hire people with diverse skills and talents who share the same entrepreneurial passion. This is a core value at Ware Malcomb, and I'm so proud of the growth so many people exhibit and enjoy as they develop with the company. We'll study these concepts in the next few chapters.

2

Self-Awareness and the Art of Leadership

"Pleasure in the job puts perfection in the work."
—Aristotle

Creatively synthesizing disparate concepts and inputs to develop whole-brained talents and skills is at the core of this book. Leonardo da Vinci was the original Renaissance man and set a great example of this idea. So we'll spend some time discussing Leonardo here.

In his book, *Lives of the Most Excellent Painters, Sculptors, and Architects*, Giorgio Vasari wrote about the artists of the 16th century. Although he knew many influential artists of the Medici Court, including Michelangelo, it's unlikely that he ever met Leonardo da Vinci. Nevertheless, Vasari wrote enthusiastically about him.

> The greatest gifts are often seen, in the course of nature, rained by celestial influences on human creatures; and sometimes, in supernatural fashion, beauty, grace, and talent are united beyond measure in one single person, in a manner that to whatever such a one turns his attention, his every action is so divine, that, surpassing all other men, it makes itself clearly known as a

thing bestowed by God (as it is), and not acquired by human art. This was seen by all mankind in Leonardo da Vinci, in whom, besides a beauty of body never sufficiently extolled, there was an infinite grace in all his actions; and so great was his genius, and such its growth, that to whatever difficulties he turned his mind, he solved them with ease.

I also agree with Walter Isaacson, who, in his monumental biography of Leonardo, saw Vasari's adulation as missing a larger point we see now through the perspective of history. "Yes, he was a genius: wildly imaginative, passionately curious, and creative across multiple disciplines. But we should be wary of that word. Slapping the 'genius' label on Leonardo oddly minimizes him by making it seem as if he was touched by lightning," Isaacson wrote.

In fact, Leonardo's vision was a human one, wrought by his own skill and ambition. It did not come from being the divine recipient, like Newton or Einstein, of a mind with so much processing power that we mere mortals cannot fathom it. Leonardo had almost no schooling and could barely read Latin or do long division. His genius was of the type we can understand, even take lessons from. It was based on skills we can aspire to improve in ourselves, such as curiosity and intense observation.[7]

Leonardo broke all the molds of his time and shaped his own persona: that of the first Renaissance man. He was not afraid to be different and explore new ideas, as known from his artistic and scientific works. His artwork often departed from traditional techniques and styles of his time. He used unconventional methods and materials, such as oil paint on plaster, which allowed him to create highly detailed and realistic images. He experimented with new perspective techniques, such as aerial angles, which gave his paintings a sense of depth and realism.

Innovative and groundbreaking ideas drove Leonardo in his scientific work. He conducted experiments on the human body, studying anatomy and physiology in great detail. He was among the first artists to ever dissect a cadaver, working on as many as 30 bodies, leaving behind a collection of accurate and powerful drawings.[8]

"He correctly described the heart as the center of the blood system and was the first to describe it as a muscle with four chambers. He discovered how small vortices of blood help shut the aortic valve, but because his scientific papers and anatomical drawings went unpublished for centuries, this mechanism wasn't confirmed until the late 1960s," a PBS *Nova* documentary revealed. "He started with an interest of understanding the body to improve his art," explains *Decoding da Vinci* producer Doug Hamilton. "But he clearly went further. He clearly became fascinated by understanding the human body."

Known as the *Portrait of a Man in Red Chalk* (c. 1510) in the Royal Library of Turin, this is widely, though not universally, accepted as a self-portrait of Leonardo da Vinci. It is thought that Leonardo drew this self-portrait at about the age of 60.

Leonardo often dissected by candlelight, taking left-handed, mirrored notes throughout the process. "There's no refrigeration; he's sometimes doing it in the dark of night," says Hamilton. "It's a messy, smelly business. And yet, when you look at his drawings, they don't convey any of that. They convey the beauty of the body."

Leonardo made numerous discoveries in physics, mechanics, and optics, and his insights into the nature of light and shadow greatly influenced the development of Renaissance art. Of the many subjects that Leonardo studied, he was particularly fascinated by the possibility of human mechanical flight. He produced more than 35,000 words and 500 sketches dealing with flying machines (he envisaged both a glider and a helicopter), the nature of air, and the flight of birds.

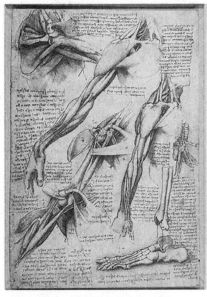

Leonardo's sketches of the muscles of the shoulder, arm, neck, and foot are shown above.

Vasari's moving words notwithstanding, while Leonardo was blessed with staggering talent, there was nothing supernatural about his passion for developing his whole self. He dared to cultivate all his abilities and skills, a model approach for improving our careers, companies, relationships, and health.[9]

Leonardo was not only an artist but someone with diverse life experiences and many skills. He didn't just build on his strengths. He had technical and theoretical training and interpersonal skills that helped him network and connect with influential people, a profound

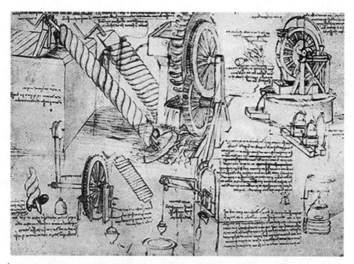

Leonardo's sketches of a water lifting device.

curiosity, and many interests in different subjects. I consider Leonardo to be the greatest genius the world has ever known.

> Leonardo was not only an artist but someone with diverse life experiences and many skills. He didn't just build on his strengths. He had technical and theoretical training and interpersonal skills that helped him network and connect with influential people, a profound curiosity, and many interests in different subjects. I consider Leonardo to be the greatest genius the world has ever known.

Being a whole-brain leader like Leonardo involves a commitment to continuous learning and layering skills: body–mind balance, formal, interpersonal and leadership, and creative.

Body–Mind Balance Skills

Leonardo is renowned for his artistic and scientific achievements, but he also had a reputation for being lean, strong, and athletic. He was known to be an excellent swimmer, particularly for long distances. Some historians claim that Leonardo was a skilled gymnast and could perform acrobatic feats such as backflips and handstands. Displays of strength attributed to Leonardo include bending horseshoes with his bare hands, a feat he used to entertain visitors to his studio.[10] For sure, some claims about Leonardo's feats may be exaggerated or based on the tall tales inspired by a famous (in the context of 16th-century Italy) artist, change agent, and innovator. For example, horseshoes and other iron implements were more pliable and softer due to primitive metallurgy.

Leonardo's horsemanship and understanding of horses, down to their anatomy, is well established. His love for horses began during childhood when he lived on his family's farm in Tuscany. He spent much time with the animals and even rode them bareback, developing an understanding of their behavior and movements. Leonardo believed that a good horseback rider should apprehend the animal's movements and behavior and have excellent balance, coordination, and control. He treated horses with kindness and respect.

Leonardo was also an accomplished archer and designed a new type of bow that was more powerful and accurate than traditional bows.

It is clear, however, that Leonardo had a keen interest in physical fitness and athleticism, which likely contributed to his overall health and well-being. In his notebooks, he wrote extensively about the benefits of exercise, proper diet, and rest for maintaining good health.

Formal Skills

The illegitimate son of a notary and a peasant girl named Caterina, Leonardo didn't come from an intellectual or cultural background and had sparse formal education growing up until he arrived in Florence. He grew up on a farm near the town of Vinci, 15 miles west of Florence. "We have very little knowledge of the first twenty years of Leonardo's life," Martin Clayton wrote in the preamble to the *The Mechanics of Man*, published by the Royal Collection Trust.

> He learned to read and write, but his arithmetical skills were always shaky; and though as an adult he tried to learn some Latin, he never became comfortable with the language of most scientific writings. Leonardo's illegitimacy prevented him from following his father into the legal profession, and he must have trained as a painter, for by 1472 he had joined the painters' guild in Florence, the Company of St Luke, and was probably working in the large studio of the great sculptor and painter Andrea del Verrocchio (1435–88).[11]

Florence had become a hub of intellectual activity and artistic exploration at the time, emerging as the birthplace of the Renaissance. Scholars and artists from around Europe came to study and participate in the exchange of evolving ideas. This intellectual ferment resulted in an evidence-based approach to knowledge that represented a radical shift in how people thought about the world. This blooming culture of inquiry profoundly impacted Leonardo, who began approaching his work with a (now renowned) sense of curiosity.

Under the guidance of Andrea del Verrocchio, Leonardo learned technical skills of drawing and painting but also the importance of observation and experimentation.

Interpersonal and Leadership Skills

When I talk about Leonardo's devotion to health and strength, most people are surprised; they are as well by his leadership abilities. Leonardo had excellent interpersonal skills and built relationships with key players in Milan and Florence. Overall, he was loyal, trustworthy, and devoted to the people around him. I have learned that these qualities are crucial to succeed as a business leader.

One notable relationship was with the Medici family, wealthy patrons of the arts and sciences in Italy. The Medicis commissioned Leonardo to design a bronze equestrian statue of their patriarch, which he never completed due to a shortage of bronze.

Leonardo forged another valuable friendship and business relationship with Ludovico Sforza, the Duke of Milan. He worked for the duke for nearly 20 years, designing and constructing various inventions, creating artwork, and organizing events. The duke also commissioned him to paint *The Last Supper*, one of Leonardo's most famous works.

Later in life, Leonardo returned to Florence and partnered with his friend and apprentice Francesco Melzi. The two worked together on various projects, including creating a treatise on painting and a new design for an ideal city. Melzi was also responsible for collecting and preserving many of Leonardo's notebooks and artwork after his death.

Whenever Leonardo noticed a problem or local royalty raised a concern wherever he happened to be, whether in Florence, Milan, or France, he would dive into this dimension of his life. Hundreds of years ahead of his time, he devised ingenious inventions, from a rotating bridge to the parachute, a flying machine, an armored car, and even a helicopter. He developed his brain in every way he could, a goal that animated his scientific and engineering creativity.

He understood that helping his allies solve problems and improve lives for the citizenry led to commissioned projects and the financial support he needed to explore the frontiers of engineering and science. Essentially, he was practicing business development.

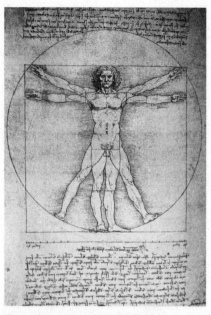

The *Vitruvian Man*, Leonardo da Vinci, 1487. The drawing depicts a male figure in two superimposed positions and simultaneously inscribed in a circle and square. The drawing and text are sometimes called the Canon of Proportions or Proportions of Man.

In one example, after the Medicis came into power in Florence, they heavily relied on an alliance with France to retain their position. In this era of Francophilia, Leonardo was tasked with creating a magnificent display to greet the new French king, Francis I, upon his arrival in Milan. He designed a life-size mechanical lion. The lion was said to have approached the king with a few heavy steps before opening its breast and spilling a myriad of lilies, or fleur-de-lis, symbolizing the French monarchy and the Florentine state. Made of wood, covered in a layer of gold leaf, designed to move and make realistic sounds, and featuring a hidden compartment to dispense flowers and other small objects, the invention stole the show.[12]

Creative Skills

Leonardo displayed another admirable quality: he did not fear his own imagination and creativity. He expressed his sense of *alta fantasia*, or high fantasy: the ability to convey imaginative expression through visual means. This belief then manifested itself in many forms. Chief among these was his two-dimensional capability with the pen or paintbrush.

From the earliest stages of his works, Leonardo would display his *fantasia* through means that were entirely inventive and novel for the time. As he brainstormed on paper, he furiously scribbled, layering different ideations and variations on top of each other, creating webs of ideas and expression. In these webs would come about new ideas, visions born out of the opaque and transparent aspects of his layered lines. He was conscious of this imaginative projection in his process: "I have in the past seen clouds and wall stains which have inspired me to beautiful inventions in many things. These stains, while wholly themselves deprived of perfection in any part, did not lack perfection in their movements or other actions."[13]

In finding this discussion during my research, I was struck by the inspiring coincidence that my son James, in his creative work, has similarly seen and captured imagery in stains and random elements in nature and the built environment. He published three books around this concept of photos as *Accidental Art*.*

From our contemporary understanding of art and artists, Leonardo's layering technique may seem fairly routine: we expect an artist to practice in this creative storm of pen and paper, finding

---

* You can check out his work at blurb.com/user/android01?filter=bookstore& profile_preview=true.

inspiration at the intersection of intention and incident. However, during Leonardo's time, this technique was unheard of.

There had been some precedent; fresco painters used rough underpaintings, sculptors formed rough models in clay or wax, and Verrocchio, Leonardo's master, was also known to sometimes draw impulsively in pen. However, nobody had conducted such extensive graphic experiments on paper as Leonardo did.

He would begin with soft, suggestive lines with chalk before amplifying the movement of emerging forms with energetic pen lines. As tangled lines converged into a spatial realization of form, light, and shadow, sometimes Leonardo himself would lose his bearings. He would add sepia wash, articulating and defining the most critical layers of the constructed image, creating clarity and hierarchy. At this point, if he still found his drawing too chaotic, he would press his lines through the sheet onto another, and the process would begin again.

Martin Kemp and other scholars have drawn connections between this method and scientific discovery:

> [Leonardo] developed an entirely novel "brainstorming" manner of drawing in which intertwined forms emerge and vanish like vortices in fluids. The illustrated sheet of experimental drawings for the *Madonna, Child, St. Anne, St. John and a Lamb* includes a water wheel! . . . His creative processes are what we would now call non linear: imagination (*fantasia*) allowed him to assemble "monsters" from the component parts of different animals. He cultivated inventive powers that worked in a fluid and turbulent manner—more openly than anyone had previously done. The motions of water justly serve as a simile for the motions of his thought.[14]

Leonardo's almost inconceivable genius in connecting biology and neuroscience to art and vice versa is explored in an article by Deco, Kemp, and Kringelbach in 2021 in *Current Biology*:

> Finding order in disorder is a hallmark of science and art. In the time of Leonardo da Vinci, the schism between science and art had yet to arise. In fact, Leonardo freely used scientific methods for his art and vice versa; for example, when he used his observations of turbulent, whirling water to guide his artistic imagination. Half a millennium later, a cornerstone of modern biology is the continuing search for order in dynamic processes. In neuroscience, the search has focused on understanding complex spacetime brain dynamics. Recently, turbulence has been shown to be a guiding principle underlying the necessary information processing, supporting Leonardo's search for order in disorder. Here, we argue that Leonardo's seminal insights have ongoing relevance for modern neuroscience.[15]

Continuous Learning and the Art of Leadership

Leonardo pursued knowledge *through* art and *in the practice of* art. His life was all about continuous learning until the day he died. Continuous learning is more than training content and conferences, though these are critical. It's how we learn about ourselves and push the limits of our potential. Leonardo is a model for understanding *what* a whole-brain leader and learner is and *why*

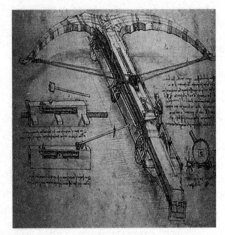

The giant catapult. Leonardo's imagination is seemingly limitless.

this approach is transformational. We can harness strengths and address our skills gaps by finding our inner Leonardo.

For me, the philosophy of layering itself, although abstract in nature, is due to Leonardo's influence and manifests in the entire concept of layers.

If your mind is open to learning from every experience *and* every person, you no longer fear what you had taught yourself to avoid. If you want to be a leader and run a business, it's important to immerse in and experience every aspect of that business— especially those parts where you are weak or uncomfortable. If you avoid them, you will not be as effective a leader as possible. You don't have to be great at everything; that's not the point. But if you're not great at P&L statements or balance sheets, at least understand them so you have some fluency and can discuss them intelligently.

> **Leonardo pursued knowledge *through* art and *in the practice of* art. His life was all about continuous learning until the day he died. Continuous learning is more than training content and conferences, though these are critical. It's how we learn about ourselves and push the limits of our potential. Leonardo is a model for understanding *what* a whole-brain leader and learner is and *why* this approach is transformational. We can harness strengths and address our skills gaps by finding our inner Leonardo.**

This strategy can be viewed through the layered leadership framework. Understand you have specific strengths and directions where you excel. Knowing and building your strengths is one layer of growth. I also challenge you to invest time and effort with creativity to see where you aren't as strong and develop those layers. Explore, experiment, and dissect your preconceptions. Then you will spark new ideas and insights to get better than you were. The more you develop yourself in all aspects of learning—art, science, business, politics, and health (diet and exercise)—the larger your impact on your organization and the world. Unrelenting curiosity is key.

How Do You Develop Your Whole Brain?

The culture at Ware Malcomb is collaborative, team oriented, and people focused. As part of this culture, we nurture continuous self-evaluation, consideration, and growth. Our continuous learning initiatives focus on skills categories or WM leadership traits and their leading attributes. Consider incorporating a similar process for you and your employees and leaders.

We help leaders assess themselves through "StrengthsFinder" as a way for each of them and the larger leadership team to understand each leader's natural strengths and how to position them in the company. But the Tinkertoy exercise is to challenge leaders to round out their skill set and develop whole-brain thinking.

The following outlines critical skills for leadership development, with each person identifying their areas for growth.

Build Your Team

- Use a collaborative, team leadership style.
- ID your successor.

- Allow others to lead.
- Develop and coach others.

Build Your Business

- Steady vision: stay out in front of your company.
- Prioritize what is best for the company over what is best for yourself.
- Communicate with passion and integrity.
- Jump in occasionally to help get the work done.
- Listen and pay attention.

Build Yourself

- Focus on growing, pushing your own limits.
- Ask for candid feedback from a trusted colleague.
- Set the example.
- Be approachable.
- Employ empathy for others.

An excellent tool (taken from my childhood) in this development process is the Tinkertoys®, a building kit invented in 1914 and still going strong, even after the advent of video games.

GETTY/ANACLETO RAPPING

I created a metaphor that uses Tinkertoys as a means to encourage a shift toward whole-brain thinking. Here's how it works:

Distribute a collection of spokes and wheels to partici-pants. Frame the process by asking how they see them-selves in the present, with spokes representing specific skill areas. Then instruct them to visualize achieving their ulti-mate potential.

Representing one's current skill assessment. PHOTO BY WARE MALCOMB.

The following seven questions prompt and guide self-discovery. Long spokes represent areas of leadership strength:

- What short spokes are on your wheel among the diverse skills and attributes discussed?
- What attributes will you develop as a result?
- What are the self-limiting beliefs that are holding you back?
- What are other limitations, beliefs internalized through industry, career experience, familial expectations, etc.?
- What limitations are you embracing that define your box of self-perceived limitations?
- What steps should you take to break out and break through?
- How can you grow your sphere of influence and learning?

Representing whole-brain development. PHOTO BY WARE MALCOMB.

It's also critical throughout the process to identify and celebrate your strengths and achievements.

No one started with a more unbalanced Tinkertoy wheel than me. Even if you are an MBA or seasoned manager, becoming a new leader means you have a lot to learn. Speaking for myself, I didn't know how to run a business when I was promoted to run the San Fernando Valley office.

Personal Development = Business Development

I was assigned to the design department when I first joined Ware Malcomb. I assisted with designs for new projects. One of the things that I was good at was staying organized and completing tasks on time. I came in early and stayed late to make sure things got done. I needed to learn what was essential to our company because my previous company had a different client base. I wanted to ensure I understood commercial real estate because that was important for sound design approaches and to serve our clients. This aptitude for bigger-picture thinking took me out of the design department. It expanded my role into project management, where I learned to run several projects and had many team members working with me on all the projects. My projects were going great, and I related well to my clients and the consultants on the team.

At this point in my career, I used the skills taught in college and internships. Staying organized was a natural skill for me, from maintaining my calendar to keeping detailed notes of client meetings, taking their feedback and implementing design revisions, and then monitoring delivery deadlines. I tried hard to give all the team members good direction and produce the projects.

I came in early and stayed late to make sure things got done. I needed to learn what was essential to our company because my previous company had a different client base. I wanted to ensure I understood commercial real estate because that was important for sound design approaches and to serve our clients. This aptitude for bigger-picture thinking took me out of the design department. It expanded my role into project management, where I learned to run several projects and had many team members working with me on all the projects.

You go to school to learn a skill, a profession. If you are good at it, you get promoted into doing something you weren't necessarily trained to do: lead people. I have some natural leadership ability, but I had to refine that a lot over time. At this point in my career, I was pretty clumsy at it. Still, my bosses could see that I was performing and committed. I ensured my projects went well and that my clients were happy, and I energized my team members. Of course, this was not always the case; I made many mistakes, but I was committed to the company and leading as well as possible.

I was offered the chance to manage and launch the San Fernando Valley branch during a company picnic. I was there with Sandy and my son James. We had driven separately because James was a baby, and you never know. Sandy decided to take off toward the end of the day, and I told her I was right behind her. I was going around to say goodbye to everyone, and Bill Malcomb said, "Hey, you got a minute before you go?" I said, "Sure."

He wanted to talk to me about a new office in North LA in Woodland Hills, in the San Fernando Valley. We were working on several large projects with one of our most important clients, The Voit

Companies. Bill and Bill wanted to establish an office in the Valley to service the client—and they wanted me to run it. Bill Malcomb described this opportunity and said, "Why don't you go home and talk to Sandy about it over the weekend?" I responded that I did not need the weekend; I was in.

So, after my first promotion, I had to study what to do, fast. I researched a few companies to learn what they did right, discern what they did wrong, and understand the pitfalls ahead. I was learning on the job, but I also studied what other terrific leaders had done before me in various areas.

The leaders I was reading about found a way, even if it meant being uncomfortable, because that was part of the job. For a business to thrive, leaders have to set an example and model the credo of their company. That instills behavior and builds culture.

First and foremost, my mission was to provide great service to Voit and build a team to deliver. But one area where I had self-doubt and discomfort was in business development. Bill and Bill and other people I spoke to confirmed that to build and stabilize the office, I needed to seek out industry partners and potential clients in the Valley beyond our great client The Voit Companies. On a daily basis, I needed to take the steps necessary to reach outside of my comfort zone, make calls, and ask people for introductions. I had to go to regional and national industry conferences to build relationships and business for us. Our competition was doing it, so I needed to too.

At first, I'd show up at an industry event, grab my badge and materials, and head into the conference. I would stand in whatever space, feel uncomfortable, and start walking around the room to find someone I knew and hang with them. I quickly realized that if you only spend time with friends and colleagues, you are not doing what you should be doing. You're in your comfort zone, but what are you accomplishing?

I did that a few times, trying to get comfortable. Then I started watching the people who were good at networking and learning from those who approached me with ease, an open posture, warm eye contact, curiosity. I noticed these people were also generous, not pumping me for favors or business.

A book on networking that helped me said that giving and finding something in common with the person you are chatting with is an approach that works over time. Lead with a giving approach. Take what is offered and be a giver in return. Follow-ups and opportunities flow organically. One mistake many people make is joining networking events and aggressively asking for business.

I took the advice of "show up and give, and it will come back to you" to heart because it resonated with my personality and conversational style. After identifying what was holding me back, I pushed forward. At events, I began to work the room slowly, attempting to meet individuals I didn't know, engage in conversation with them, and explore ways we could assist each other. That was my whole attitude. Then I expanded my sphere of influence and effectiveness. As I overcame my discomfort and worked the room on a regular basis, windows suddenly opened for business development. It became muscle memory. When the moment was right, asking for work was much easier.

I remember taking our current president, Jay Todisco, to his first business development event many years ago. We'd hired Jay for a leadership position in our Irvine office, and Jay's an excellent architect. He hadn't been out on the circuit in his last job, but Jay is outgoing and gregarious. When we told him that business development was part of his responsibility, he was tentative, but he took to it quickly. I remember the first time I took him to a networking event: We walked in, and I said, "Okay, let's talk for a few minutes, speak to a couple of people, and then we will split up. We will work around the room and do our best. Then we will recalibrate, see what we learned, talk to a few more people, and get out of here."

Of course, he was much more of a natural than I ever was. He did a great job. He became our preeminent partner in all things business development and teaches our people how to approach and master it. He and Ted Heisler (our VP of interior architecture and design) created a curriculum called BD 101, with which they have trained dozens of our staff on the basics of business development.

Hiring

As with many managers, I had to learn the hard way that you should hire slowly and fire fast. In the early years, I hired well at times and *not* so well at others. Over time, we adopted interview and screening techniques, bringing us a top-tier workforce of amazingly committed professionals. But we had to experience the pain of figuring that all out.

> **As with many managers, I had to learn the hard way that you should hire slowly and fire fast. In the early years, I hired well at times and *not* so well at others. Over time, we adopted interview and screening techniques, bringing us a top-tier workforce of amazingly committed professionals. But we had to experience the pain of figuring that all out.**

Sometimes I was too hard on people early in the San Fernando Valley office because I expected everybody to have the same attitude as me and they often did not. I had to learn that people can do great work but may have different ambitions or aspirations than me, because their life situations require that. Early on as a young leader eager to prove myself, I may have pushed clients too hard for more business or faster approvals and had to walk back a few comments. My goal was to learn and get better all the time. Learn from your mistakes, of course, but learn *fast*.

We did assemble an incredible team of architects and designers who produced great projects, serviced the clients, made money for the company, and advanced their careers.

Any of you moving into a senior role will need to prepare for, or have already experienced, needing to conquer the frontier of financial statements and balance sheets.

We won't be seeing the paper boy on his bicycle route again, but being one taught me a lot. GENERATED WITH BING AI IMAGE, POWERED BY DALL-E.

Math is one of my strengths, and I first learned how profits worked as a kid on my paper route. I had to collect monthly subscription fees door-to-door from customers to pay my distributor no matter what. If I didn't collect from all of my customers, I still had to pay the distributor for all the papers I delivered. The money left in my pocket would be mainly up to me based on how good I was at doing my job. Profits went down if collections declined. When I started learning the profit and loss statements at WM, although it was simplified by comparison, my paper route helped me with the basic concept. While the bicycle kid paper route is lost to the past, people including Warren Buffett, Tom Cruise, and Walt Disney credit working their paper route with invaluable insights about business, thrift, and profits.

Math is one of my strengths, and I first learned how profits worked as a kid on my paper route. I had to collect monthly subscription fees door-to-door from customers to pay my distributor no matter what. If I didn't collect from all of my customers, I still had to pay the distributor for all the papers I delivered. The money left in my pocket would be mainly up to me based on how good I was at doing my job. Profits went down if collections declined. When I started learning the profit and loss statements at WM, although it was simplified by comparison, my paper route helped me with the basic concept. While the bicycle kid paper route is lost to the past, people including Warren Buffett, Tom Cruise, and Walt Disney credit working their paper route with invaluable insights about business, thrift, and profits.

Before my promotion at Ware Malcomb, my knowledge of managing business finances was limited to what I learned from my paper route. My understanding of profit and loss was only at a basic level.

When I first started managing an office, and later when I was responsible for the financials of the entire company, I found it important to learn how to analyze and interpret profit and loss statements and balance sheets. I sought guidance from individuals such as Bill and Bill, as well as our consulting accountant, Ken Kubota, and asked many questions to gain a better understanding. To fully comprehend what led to a robust balance sheet or financial statement, I dedicated a considerable amount of time each month to studying these documents.

This proved particularly crucial when we were hit with a difficult recession in 1992. It was quite a challenge for us to catch up with the financials and come up with ways to cut down on costs, such as rent and salaries. Our biggest expense was the team, who were also our most valuable asset, and it was difficult to decide on lay-offs and reduced hours. We were aware that such decisions would have a significant impact on people's lives, but tough choices had to be made to save jobs and ensure the company's survival.

Ultimately, a recession provides invaluable lessons you can't learn at any other time, and we made the necessary cuts to save the company. It was a tough learning experience, but it taught me what we needed to know to keep our business solid and healthy going forward.

CFO Tobin Sloane and I have spent hours at a time discussing the dimensions of this challenge. "Over the course of my 20 years at Ware Malcomb," Sloane told me, "I've learned that dealing with the economy can be a tricky business. It's not just about numbers on a page; it's about people's livelihoods and the health of our company. We know that the economy can be unpredictable, which is why we always seek out the best information available to under-stand its trajectory and impact on our business lines and regions. It's not always easy to make decisions about staffing levels, but it's crucial to our success. We understand that these decisions can have a personal impact on our staff, but we also know that keeping the company healthy is essential for everyone's stability and longevity. In my experience, it's always best to be proactive when it comes to staffing decisions. Delaying action only makes existing challenges worse, which is why we've always made timely decisions about staffing. It's not just about immediate stability; it's about ensuring that we can continue to compete and thrive even when things get tough. We know that these decisions are never easy, but we also know that they're necessary for the long-term health of our company and the people who work here."

Over the years, I continued to learn about topics including personnel, insurance, consultants, efficiency, and quality control. That was a great learning experience for me and formed the basis for business concepts that I have taught the leaders in our firm.

In layered leadership, I urge you to remember, don't squeeze out the seams of joy and satisfaction that drew you to your profession or the everyday satisfactions of doing a job well, of collaborating and knocking down obstacles with your team, whatever you do. (Misery doesn't often lead to success.)

A few practices nurture joy and creativity beyond what we've discussed: give yourself the freedom to fail when innovating, empower yourself to reimagine your work product or process and prove it works, help your team members when needed, and, importantly, don't overschedule. You need exploration and planning time for those flashes of light to be seen. Allow others to fail and take risks in pursuit of growth. Don't play "schedule Tetris" as Jeremy Utley and Perry Klebahn put it in *HBR*,[16] "cramming every possible incoming meeting invite into every single opening, as if finding space for every meeting were the point of the game . . . The most visionary leaders block time for unscheduled time." I find that creative thought (flashes of light) invariably occurs from unscheduled, relaxed moments. Recreational and fitness activities you love provide meditative peace and relief from stress, and nourish the imagination.

Among the things I love about architecture and design is that it draws on the whole brain—various kinds of intelligence. And there's always a narrative, like cinema. There are lots of twists and turns. Suddenly a roadblock goes up: the city doesn't like an aspect of the design during the entitlement process, the construction costs are too high, or consultants don't talk to each other as much as they should. Sometimes the drawings aren't coordinated as well as they are supposed to be. Sometimes you have to just get out into the field and meet the contractors during construction. You may need to visit the building site to deal with a field issue.

Conditions come up that no one has anticipated but you have to solve: supply chain issues, weather delays, and labor shortages. You encounter all manner of challenges along the way, but you reach an ending to that particular story when the building is completed, and people live and work there. That's what makes it an interesting, challenging, and rewarding profession. You helped create something that people and their lives or careers will be shaped by.

Developing our capabilities, nurturing our joy, and finding the creative spark in whatever our day brings—these layers synthesize into the wholeness of leadership. One of the great writers, Pearl S. Buck, said: "The secret of joy in work is contained in one word—excellence. To know how to do something well is to enjoy it."

All of the concepts we are talking about form layers and synthesize into whole-brain thought, this wholeness of leadership, somehow.

That manifests in flashes of light, whether in my art or Ware Malcomb. It's the same process for thinking about the company, solving a problem that exists, or having a vision for the future where this company needs to go. These thought processes weave into a complete idea of the company.

Okay, a homework assignment. In your Exploration Sketchbook, write down the seven questions, and identify a skills gap on your leadership wheel that you want to begin closing and how. Be honest—it's a private exercise.

Then, over a few weeks, note your progress—and any ideas that arise. As you progress along a pathway, continue writing, sketching, even collecting physical objects related to your whole-brain thinking.

Developing Others and the Pivot to Leadership

"Above all, it is necessary to recognize that knowledge cannot be pumped into human beings the way grease is forced into a machine. The individual may learn; he is not taught."

—Douglas McGregor

We can trace the history of leadership back to ancient civilizations, where the need for coordination and organization arose in various human endeavors. Ancient civilizations such as the Egyptians, Mesopotamians, and Greeks required coordination and organization for building monumental structures, managing agriculture, and conducting military operations. (Those ancient architects did some amazing work.)* Socrates himself is believed to have said

---

* See the 2005 book by architect Craig B. Smith entitled *How the Great Pyramid Was Built*, https://www.amazon.com/HowGreatPyramidWasBuilt /dp/158834200X. A case study in project management from an architect's point of view, the book contains forensic analysis of the Great Pyramid's construction and planning. In the book, Smith details the program management of the Great Pyramid 4,500 years ago. He provides an interesting history of the culture and lifestyle of the builders and explains the mathematics of the engineering, but the crux of the book is Smith's perspective of the Great Pyramid as a large, well-planned public works project.

that leading is a competency distinct from possessing technical skills and knowledge.

For sure, orchestrating men, materials, and operations on a large scale remained the realm of kings, wealthy landowners, and warlords for over a thousand years. While many impressive temples, aqueducts, roads, and monuments were built, labor was usually provided by conscription and chattel slavery.

1926, Stereograph of camels and men at the base of the Great Pyramid at Cheops, an ancient marvel of management. LIBRARY OF CONGRESS, PUBLIC DOMAIN. MEADVILLE, PA.: KEYSTONE VIEW CO.

In the Middle Ages, production was done at a small scale, and as a result, very little management was required compared to the current era.

The Renaissance witnessed the emergence of several notable master builders who made significant contributions to architecture and engineering. Filippo Brunelleschi built the dome of the Florence Cathedral, and Leon Battista Alberti wrote the influential treatise *De re aedificatoria*.* Donato Bramante designed St. Peter's Basilica in Rome, while Michelangelo Buonarroti designed the Laurentian Library in Florence. Andrea Palladio is widely regarded

---

* *On the Art of Building* is a renowned architectural treatise, the first theoretical book on architecture to be written in the Italian Renaissance. In 1485, it became the first printed book on architecture, and was followed a year later by the first printed edition of Vitruvius.

as one of the most influential figures in architectural history. These masters left a legacy that continues to inspire architects, students, and art historians, among many.

The rise of factories and large-scale manufacturing necessitated new approaches to managing people, resources, and processes. However, many managers viewed their workers as machinery, or worse—at least machines were maintained. Child labor was commonplace. As noted by the historians at the US Library of Congress:

> For millions of working Americans, the Industrial Revolution changed the very nature of their daily work. Previously, they might have worked for themselves at home, in a small shop, or outdoors, crafting raw materials into products, or growing a crop from seed to table. When they took factory jobs, they were working for a large company. The repetitive work often involved only one small step in the manufacturing process, so the worker did not see or appreciate what was being made; the work was often dangerous and performed in unsanitary conditions. Some women entered the workforce, as did many children. Child labor became a significant issue.
>
> The new jobs for the working class were in the cities. Thus, the Industrial Revolution began the transition of the United States from a rural to an urban society. Young people raised on farms saw greater opportunities in the cities and moved there, as did millions of immigrants from Europe. Providing housing for all the new residents of cities was a problem, and many workers found themselves living in urban slums; open sewers ran alongside the streets, and the water supply was often tainted, causing disease. These deplorable urban conditions gave rise to the Progressive Movement in the early twentieth century; the result would be

many new laws to protect and support people, eventually changing the relationship between government and the people.

These economic and social factors resulted in tectonic shifts in management.

Many industrialists driving the American economy failed because they did not consider their employees to be people who could also be their customers (Henry Ford's genius was to realize this truth).

It wasn't until the Industrial Revolution in the 1800s that formal management became necessary with the emergence of mass production. This was a massive shift in the history of the United States and the world.

In the late 19th and early 20th centuries, Frederick Taylor showed up with his stopwatch and introduced the concept of scientific management. Taylor focused on increasing efficiency by optimizing work processes, standardizing tasks, and conducting time-motion studies to improve productivity. Taylorism had many lasting influences, but employee engagement and motivation were not among them.

As the scientific measurement method dehumanized workers while demanding increasing productivity, the conflict between labor and management was inevitable. This conflict resulted in the emergence of the personnel department (an ancestor of the HR department) as a method to slow down unions, reduce turnover, and acknowledge workers' needs.

During this period, the idea was that productivity would increase if work were more exciting and rewarding. MIT professor Douglas McGregor worked closely with Abraham Maslow and carried out research in employee psychology. McGregor believed in developing management practices that sought to operate from the basis of an understanding of the worker. He felt that it was management's job to provide work to their employees that gave them a sense of self-actualization and worth. He argued that more enlightened management practices would simultaneously achieve the goals of both the organization and the employees.

In management history, McGregor identified two approaches to motivating employees: one involves authoritative direction and top-down control, while the other emphasizes employees' sense of accomplishment, ownership, and self-control. These approaches are known as Theory X and Theory Y, respectively. Warren Bennis, a renowned leadership expert, author, and educator, once remarked that we all, knowingly or not, owe a debt to McGregor, much as economists do to Keynes.

Peter Drucker is widely respected as the pioneer of many modern management strategies. Among these, his most renowned is the concept of MBO (management by objectives). The MBO approach involves setting realistic and objective goals, communicating them to the employees responsible for achieving them, and appropriately dividing the responsibility for their accomplishment. Management's role is to provide support, monitor progress, and evaluate performance, intervening when necessary to correct any issues that arise. If the goals are met or exceeded, all share the profits. Moreover, Drucker contends that a business's purpose is to generate customers and that marketing and innovation are the two critical functions to achieve that end.

In Search of Excellence became the breakthrough phenomenon that launched Theory Y mainstream and established leadership as a popular reading topic. Written by Thomas J. Peters and Robert H. Waterman Jr. and published in 1982, it quickly became a bestseller. The book focuses on the study of 43 successful American companies. The well-managed companies were largely built on the earlier ideas of McGregor and Herzberg.

In Search of Excellence emphasized the importance of organizational culture, leadership, and employee engagement in achieving long-term success. It is one of the most influential nonfiction books in modern history.

Others, of course, also made lasting contributions to modern management thinking. Stephen Covey's *The 7 Habits of Highly Successful People*, Peter Senge's *The Fifth Discipline*, and Jim Collins and Jerry Porras's *Built to Last* are among bestselling books on management principles.

Among the iconic thinkers of this era was Michael Porter, based at Harvard Business School. Throughout his illustrious career, Porter explored ways in which organizations can achieve a long-term competitive edge. While summarizing his vast body of work is challenging, Porter suggested that there are three ways for a firm to gain such an advantage. First, they can opt for cost-based leadership by becoming the lowest-cost producer. Second, they can offer a differentiated product or service for which a customer is willing to pay a premium price, thus achieving value-added leadership. Lastly, they can compete in a niche market with laser-like focus. The second and third factors identified by Porter play a crucial role in the success of Ware Malcomb.

For decades, this shifting pantheon of influential management thinkers and corporate practitioners drove the development of corporate leadership. Now, change never, ever stops. In the words of management historians Robert Lloyd and Wayne Aho, "Managers in the 21st century must confront challenges their counterparts of even a few years ago could hardly imagine. The ever growing wave of technology, the impact of artificial intelligence, the evolving nature of globalization, and the push pull tug of war between the firm's stakeholder and shareholder interests are chief among the demands today's managers will face."[17]

I believe that excellence in your organization is no longer defined from the C-suite by one management "school" or guru. At Ware Malcomb, we are a learning organization and a Theory Y organization. We adopted Jack Welch's vision for a leadership academy. We've learned how to swim in blue oceans.

These six books were formative and influential in the strategies I developed for Ware Malcomb and our leaders.

We have a strong focus on our markets and manage efficient operations systems, allowing time and resources for innovation and flashes of light. Layered leadership is about strategies moving and reforming themselves, with employee contributions becoming a catalyst for that evolution. It's about drawing on a selection of approaches and nailing them into a framework. Just as the best MLB baseball teams now draw on *Moneyball* advanced analytical data, sports science, *and* more traditional techniques (such as hitting the opposite way) as best suits their players, so it is true of your company.

Layered leadership is about strategies moving and reforming themselves, with employee contributions becoming a catalyst for that evolution. It's about drawing on a selection of approaches and nailing them into a framework. Just as the best MLB baseball teams now draw on *Moneyball* advanced analytical data, sports science, *and* more traditional techniques (such as hitting the opposite way) as best suits their players, so it is true of your company.

At Ware Malcomb, we allow every employee to participate in shaping the company's goals. We nurture generative innovation where new ideas are always percolating. It's not top down, nor is it bottom up, but a synthesis of both.

Our mentorship program, leadership meetings, and other vehicles (more on these processes later in the chapter) open several opportunities for executives, designers, operations managers, and team members to share ideas.

The quality of these ideas never fails to impress. Our senior leadership team meets a few times yearly to curate and work on the suggestions from throughout the firm. After winnowing down the roster of ideas, they are fed into the strategic plans for each office and the larger company. These documents then are aligned and deployed as a road map to guide the company and regional offices through the year. We also benchmark ourselves against the road map on a quarterly basis.

I'll explain further how open sourcing our strategy drives how we evaluate our progress and identify what we need to build upon for the following year. We also anticipate what our roadblocks and challenges are going to be and strategize around them. We don't anticipate every roadblock, but we tend not to get blindsided either.

We've evolved this methodology over many years, refining and improving it, but the concepts are still the same as when we started the process decades ago. Our autonomy, commitment to developing people, and interest in new ideas no matter where they come from make us enormously attractive to new hires and new clients. That gives us a competitive advantage. *We don't measure ourselves against our industry so much as against other great businesses.*

Our progress also came about because my former partner Jim and I worked hard to build a productive relationship that allowed us to bring our creativity and ideas to the table to work through. We had a fantastic partnership.

Jim retired far before I did, but we became a powerful double team—able to anticipate the next smart move during our tenure.

I saw Jim one weekend in March 2023 when we had an open house for our office in Denver. We were catching up, looking around at the amazing designs and excited team members and friends. We mostly shared an awestruck semi-disbelief at how Ware Malcomb became such a great company. We talked about how when we took over the company, we had fewer than 30 people and billed, I will never forget it, $3.2 million in 1992. In 2022, we billed $221 million and employed about a thousand people at 28 offices. Throughout our history, there have been countless stories and notable individuals, yet one truth has remained constant. Jim and I were given a mind-blowing opportunity, and we knew we wanted to do the most we could with this opportunity and provide as many people as possible a chance to grow in their careers. Inviting those opportunities for people to develop with us has been one of the main drivers of our growth.

I want you to enjoy the exponential benefits of this commitment and engagement. But it won't happen without a top-to-bottom allegiance to developing the people who contribute to your company's mission every day. Leadership is the work of understanding people with different backgrounds than you, listening instead to other points of view, and developing awareness of what your employees need to flourish. That's the critical work of this chapter: devising strategies for human development and infusing them into the culture. This chapter will provide detailed guidance for:

- mentoring that is formal but flexible;
- effective leadership meetings;
- developing a "Number Two";
- and deploying the Chessboard.

Investing in employee development is also essential to understanding and exceeding customer expectations—a relationship borne out by customer experience experts such as Joseph Michelli, Don Peppers, and Fred Reichheld. "Notions like 'customers rule' or 'employees are #1' are well-intentioned but myopic," bestselling author Michelli wrote. "I would err on the side of committing to deliver to meet the functional and emotional needs of people—whether those people are on your team or paying customers. If you are a great experience provider, your people will want to buy your products, and in that instance, they are both your team and your customer. The relationship between employee engagement and customer engagement is strong and reciprocal."[18]

Leadership is the hub of our commitment to educating and developing team members, and GE under the late Jack Welch became a role model for us. Welch retired from General Electric in 2001, and over the years his legacy has weathered criticism, but Jack Welch still has a great deal to teach us. He preached and practiced curiosity, which we need even more in the 2020s. GE's leadership education programs and culture of executive improvement inspired CEOs worldwide, including this author. Additionally, Welch's embrace of earnings, efficiency, and productivity over fuzzier aspirations was widely adopted by business schools and management consultants as the foundation of American capitalism.

Leadership scholars, including Claudio Fernández-Aráoz, Boris Groysberg, and Tricia Gregg, have conducted studies showing that a relentless thirst for knowledge is essential. Leaders cannot afford to have outdated skill sets and must constantly seek knowledge. Welch was ahead of the game in this regard. "His curiosity, candor, and focus on making the right people decisions ensure that he remains a role model," Fernández-Aráoz wrote for *Harvard Business Review*. "These are three aspects of effective leadership that we should all seek to cultivate."[19]

A Mentoring Ethos

Mentoring is not a bolt-on or afterthought for businesses today. It is inseparable from everything you do. Mentoring is a valuable relationship in which a more experienced individual (the mentor) provides guidance, support, and advice to a less experienced individual (the mentee). Effective mentoring can have a significant impact on personal and professional growth.

In the 1990s, Jim and I started encouraging mentoring on an informal basis, as we tried to guide and coach young leaders that we brought into the company into our ways of doing things. For many years, we did that, and later when I built my executive team. I mentored all of them, writing quick notes for each person I would keep in my sketchbook, and following up with them on certain issues (Jack Welch referenced this practice in his books).

In the 1990s, Jim and I started encouraging mentoring on an informal basis, as we tried to guide and coach young leaders that we brought into the company into our ways of doing things. For many years, we did that, and later when I built my executive team. I mentored all of them, writing quick notes for each person I would keep in my sketchbook, and following up with them on certain issues (Jack Welch referenced this practice in his books).

In the early 2000s, Ware Malcomb's Vice President of Strategic Initiatives, Ruth Brajevich, suggested we start a more formalized mentoring program that would engage everyone at every level in the company. This evolved into the WM Mentoring Coaching program, rooted in the concept that anyone at any level can get mentored, with senior managers mentored by the top leadership. It became popular and still is. "The initiative had a great deal of support after one of our leadership retreats, and was something a lot of our people were asking for," Ruth said in an interview for this book.

12.22.14.

Dear Coony,

What a great year for the Pleasanton office. Congratulations! Great revenue & profit, teamwork & customer service (& the move!) Thanks for your leadership in the office leaders meetings and the WM Foundation, and your ongoing participation in IAG. Next year I would like to see you focus on:

1. SF – Profitability & market share.
2. Diversification in Pleasanton – now is the time to get stronger.
3. Think about whether you would like to take responsibility for Seattle. We'll discuss in January.

Great year Coony, awesome job! Thanks for everything!

Larry

international reach
wareonableamb.com
architecture | planning | interiors   10 edelman
graphics | civil engineering   irvine. ca 92618
p 949.660.9128
f 949.863.1581

12.21.15.

Dear Ted,

Congratulations on another good year for Irvine Interiors. Better market share & profits, helped you this year. Also thanks for your continued leadership of IAC, work on corporate accounts & participation on the Executive Team. Next year we need to make significant progress on:

1. Revenue growth/(biz dev!) & market share in OC & IE.
2. Much more market share in landlord accounts! (see last year's note).
3. Specific goals & progress with corporate accounts.
4. Finishing action items in IAG.

Thanks for a great year Ted, awesome job! Thanks,

Larry

international reach
wareonableamb.com
architecture | planning | interiors   10 edelman
graphics | civil engineering   irvine. ca 92618
p 949.660.9128
f 949.863.1581

12.21.16.

Dear Tobin,

Thanks for all of your amazing contributions to WM this year. Your team is making a great transition to serving the offices well. Your insight on the board is important and valuable. You've accomplished a lot this year, and there is always more to do:

1. Refine internal processes to add monthly deadlines that are communicated to office leaders (billings, contract terms) etc.
2. Individual office recession plans.
3. Real estate plans – proactive – assign a team member to manage leases.
4. WM 4.0 – accounting related clunky issues to smooth out.

Great job and thanks for everything this year.

Larry

international reach
wareonableamb.com
architecture | planning | interiors   10 edelman
graphics | civil engineering   irvine. ca 92618
p 949.660.9128
f 949.863.1581

Examples of my year-end notes to leaders.

Many companies mentor; of course, we are not unique. But we've put our hearts and total support into improving and refining this program over many years.

Mentoring is an essential part of Ware Malcomb's work culture, and it benefits everyone who sees its value (which is almost everybody). This practice is founded on trust and helps establish further trust within the team. Furthermore, it enhances both personal and professional development, and it acts as an excellent social glue for your team. Mentoring also allows for a shorter learning curve, which means that people can improve their skills faster and make better decisions upstream of a client deadline, rather than downstream, which can be costly and time consuming. "Mentoring helped us connect our leadership to our people," said Ruth. "After the Great Recession of 2008 there was a big gap. Our mentors learn a lot about the young generations and what is important to them. There is mutual benefit."

Mentoring is a concept we had from the beginning. We want to help people develop their careers here in the way that they want to take their career, what's attractive to them, what they are passionate about. Mentoring is part of how we help them set goals and achieve them. It's a part of our company philosophy, and we continue to develop the program.

Over time we have added outside coaches to help our top leaders. That has also been very successful because it aligns with the company values we want. We care about our people. We want them to believe they can succeed here and pursue their passions and career goals. It's also rewarding for the mentor. It's enjoyable. I scaled my mentoring back quite a bit because my role has shifted, but I still mentor a few people and have at least one formal assignment in 2024 that I am mentoring. I do it because I love it and know it works.

Our analysis of the success factors in our program confirms the findings of many credible experts: senior management buy-in, mentor–mentee chemistry, intentionality, clarity of goals on the part of mentees, monitoring, accountability, and commitment by everyone involved.

In one study, Deloitte identified variables that correlate with success:

Mentoring relationships should be mutually beneficial; mentees receive valuable career advice, while mentors invest in the strength of their organization. Formal mentorship programs should use professional and personal aspirations as criteria to match employees with mentors . . .

Mentoring promotes diversity by providing equal opportunities for every employee to develop and advance professionally. It helps organizations identify high-potential employees and ensures they are provided with the resources they need to develop and feel supported.[20]

And a 2018 Deloitte blog post spelled out what comprises an effective mentoring system:

For starters, implementing this type of program within an organization requires senior management buy in, awareness around the benefits and needs of the program, proper accountability as well as a clear process and guidelines in place to define the requirements from all parties involved. It also requires having mentors and mentees that want to participate willingly, mentors with the right expertise, and the openness and eagerness from both parties to learn.[21]

I want to make a further essential point. Pairing non-direct reports with mentors is far more effective, allowing more openness and objective feedback and providing opportunities to develop relationships outside the reporting structure. We layer and synthesize particular methods and concepts to continuously improve our mentoring and related initiatives.

A. Mentee Sets Long- and Short-Term Goals

We like to ensure mentees are responsible for setting goals and communicating their short- and long-term goals that their mentor can review with them. Written goals are essential. They should be hard to reach and require commitment and consistency to achieve.

The mentee should identify particular roadblocks that they are having or anticipate having. Leave the agenda primarily to the mentee with guidance from the mentor. The mentee starts the process with dialogue along the lines of "Here's what I am trying to do; here are the barriers. I have some suggestions for next steps and would love your input on these." It's not about the day-to-day work that a person reviews with their supervisor. It's more about career building and developing as a professional and a person, giving the mentor a solid agenda to work with their counterpart.

Every employee will have concerns about their career; while roadblocks can be discouraging, they are not insurmountable. With perseverance, proactive strategies, and a willingness to learn and grow, individuals can navigate these career obstacles: a formal mentor program accelerates this process for your employees, who will want to build their future with your firm.

> **Every employee will have concerns about their career; while roadblocks can be discouraging, they are not insurmountable. With perseverance, proactive strategies, and a willingness to learn and grow, individuals can navigate these career obstacles: a formal mentor program accelerates this process for your employees, who will want to build their future with your firm.**

B. Maintain a Rhythm

The mentoring process will be most effective when the counterparts find the rhythm and timing that works for them. However, it requires that they agree on regular get-togethers. We recommend meeting monthly; some people do it more frequently with shorter sessions. Everybody has their little tweaks to it. The point is to care about the mentee's success and help them navigate.

C. Find and Foster Creativity and Trust

What has Ware Malcomb's experience proven practical regarding best practices for mentors? First, agree with and confirm your mentee's goals and ensure you are aligned. Write them down and keep up to date. Mentors can check on goal progress and make adjustments. Encourage your mentee to explore new ideas, seek out challenging assignments, and engage in continuous learning. In my sessions, I will suggest books or courses to check out, inspiring and awesome places to visit and nurture the soul, ways to have fun and de-stress.

Second, I find less is more when transmitting my experiences and views to build rapport and trust. Listen actively, mirror back what your mentee shares, respect confidentiality, pose questions rather than state the obvious, and allow your colleagues to discover their ideas. Mentors need to listen and step back but know when to provide constructive feedback and guidance to help their mentees identify their strengths, weaknesses, and areas for improvement. Note achievements and point out areas for growth.

Remember that mentoring is a partnership, not a directive relationship. Respect your mentee's autonomy and allow them to make their own decisions and choices. Offer guidance and support without imposing your views.

Above all, mentors are role models. Demonstrate professionalism, integrity, and ethical behavior in your own actions. Lead by example and share your experiences, lessons learned, and best practices to inspire and guide your mentee. Part of this is checking your own effectiveness and adjusting as needed. Seek feedback from your mentees to understand their experience and make improvements to the mentoring relationship.

Again, maintain regular communication. Establish a consistent meeting schedule to maintain momentum and continuity in the mentoring relationship. Regularly check in with your mentee to provide support, answer questions, and track progress. And don't forget to celebrate. Acknowledge and celebrate your mentee's milestones and accomplishments. Recognize their efforts and provide positive reinforcement, which can enhance motivation and confidence.

How to Run Great Leadership Meetings

Ware Malcomb has held leadership meetings three times a year since circa 1995, a few years after Jim and I were promoted. The idea came to me in a modest flash of light: *Let's get the senior leaders in one room for a few hours to ensure we were all going in the same direction*, I thought. *Let's talk about the company's goals, what we are pushing for, review our metrics, and start planning for the year ahead.* When we started, we were six young leaders in the Ware Malcomb conference room. In 2024, we held three WM Advance meetings with over 100 people (out of a company of 1,000). (Always in a cool conference venue—it has to be cool; we're designers!)

Each lasts all day with leaders flown in from around the Americas. We have an evening social activity after the meeting, and attendees leave the next day.

The flow of ideas and infusion of our values matters to who we are as a company. We do this to develop our leaders and teamwork across the platform. You may be thinking about the expense and time required, and you're right. It's a trade-off and one we've pondered over the years. It's not even close. The benefits of alignment, relationship building, and team enthusiasm toward the goal are indisputable.

The executive team did sensational work in advancing our leadership conference and how it has evolved. The ideas, communication, and camaraderie keep the geographically dispersed company sailing in the same direction.

Let's explore why regular leadership meetings can work for you and your organization. Leadership retreats are common and familiar with their pursuit of team building and strategic planning; what are the differentiating factors derived from our model?

Unity and alignment

You've read about the fleet of ships. I launched the metaphor at one of these meetings as an opportunity for leaders to improve communication and alignment. It's about sharing information, identifying objectives, and aligning priorities. It's about unity and a shared understanding of vision and mission. Working together. Supporting each other. Shifting quickly together when needed.

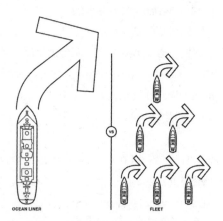

Build a team of leaders that learn how to steer toward big goals independently but in unison.

It is where our regional leaders and the executive team learned how to operate as a fleet of ships, share insights, and build strategies so we are ready to respond and change course as necessary. I saw that many of the giants in our industry operated like a colossal ocean liner that needs time to move in a new direction. A fleet of smaller vessels all going in the same direction can move quicker, and nimbler, when course corrections are needed.

Leaders Lead

One of the best ways to introduce new concepts and strategic directions is through a focused retreat where people can gather in person. This retreat allows for knowledge sharing through various methods, including speaking opportunities, breakout sessions, design presentations, informal conversations, and a structured feedback process. During an all-hands meeting, we establish long-range goals for the company, such as diversifying our product lines to ensure stability during economic downturns. We will divide into smaller groups to strategize solutions to this and other challenges facing our company to achieve these goals.

These meetings also allow leaders to share updates and lead discussions on various topics and initiatives. It's important to give everyone a chance to participate by rotating breakout and discussion leaders over time, rather than limiting these opportunities to only top executives.

Strategic Planning

By stepping away from day-to-day operations and distractions, your leaders can focus on analyzing where you are, evaluating market trends, and formulating strategies for where you want to be. Our leadership conference provides uninterrupted time and space to brainstorm, exchange ideas, and develop innovative approaches to business challenges. Typically, we start the day with a thematic motivational talk, review financials, and discuss the agenda. Our VP of Design, Jinger Tapia, will present an update of new designs from around the company. Or we will see an innovation our civil engineering group is implementing. It's good for people to know what's happening around the company.

Our leadership meetings provide an opportunity for leaders across WM to foster stronger relationships with one another, which consistently receives the highest praise in our post-meeting surveys. These meetings are crucial in promoting a unified "One Team" leadership culture.

Building the Mind Map

In one of the annual meetings, we build the mind map, which is part of our strategic planning process.

In a mind map, the central topic is placed at the center of the page or screen, and related subtopics radiate out from it in a hierarchical or interconnected structure. The subtopics can further branch out into sub-subtopics, forming a treelike structure. Each branch or subtopic is typically represented by a word or short phrase, accompanied by relevant images, symbols, or colors to aid in memory and understanding.

The key to a practical mind map is to capture information in a way that helps you generate insights, make connections, and understand complex topics more quickly. Mind maps encourage nonlinear thinking and provide a visual overview of complex information, making it easier to see relationships between ideas. They can be created on paper using pens, markers, digital tools, and software specifically designed for mind mapping. The mind map is part of our strategic plan developed over the year, then tested, amplified, refined, and polished with the open-source contributions we receive at the meeting. Adding the mind map to an existing strategic plan in process was suggested by Ruth and has only improved thanks to the leadership team. The leadership team collaborates on forming the company's mind map, the strategic plan's visualization. We used to build the mind map in the session but now we have too many people. We typically send out the overall map, and every office does one on their own that builds into the company one. And so every employee in the company has the opportunity to participate in building the mind map.

> **The mind map is part of our strategic plan developed over the year where goals are identified for various business units, departments, and initiatives, then tested, amplified, refined, and polished with the open-source contributions we receive at the meeting.**

Steps in building mind maps at the small-team, regional, and company-wide scale:

- If your company lacks designers or architects, hire a consultant to implement and guide the mapmaking. Remember that various digital tools, such as MindMeister, Xmind, or even basic drawing or diagramming software, are available for creating mind maps.
- Progress from the company-wide map to smaller business groups or departments.
- Aim for five to seven main branches per map with smaller offshoots. These branches can represent different aspects of your corporate structure, such as departments, teams, goals, or strategies. They should include financial, business diversification, development, operational, and cultural goals. Write each branch as a keyword or short phrase around the central topic.

- Identify relationships, dependencies, or interactions between different aspects of your corporate structure or strategy. Look for connections between different branches and sub-branches. Using lines or connectors to link related ideas creates a more comprehensive overview.

- Review and refine to ensure that your mind map represents a clear and logical structure, with all the relevant information captured. Adjust and refine the layout, hierarchy, or content as needed to improve clarity and readability. Share, and update . . . as needed.

- Curate. Not every idea belongs on the mind map.

There are outstanding examples of mind maps on the following page to inspire you and your team!

The Indispensable Number Two

A legendary catchphrase in television is from *Star Trek: The Next Generation*'s Patrick Stewart playing Commander Picard. "Make it so, number one," Picard says when he turns to his second in command, Commander Riker (Jonathan Frakes), with an urgent order.

Picard was onto an excellent management insight. Our numbering system is different, but the concept is the same.

At Ware Malcomb, every leader is encouraged and expected to develop or hire a second in command (#2 or Number Two). I strongly believe in this concept when it comes to developing people. Ken Wink, our current CEO, was once my Number Two for several years, and he ran daily operations at an exceptional level. Whenever I needed something done that I couldn't do myself or he

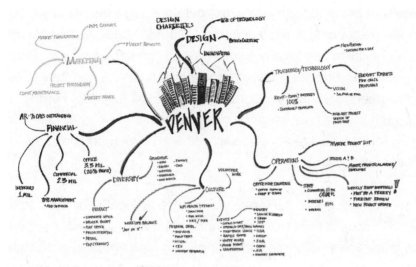

Example: Ware Malcomb Denver Mind Map.

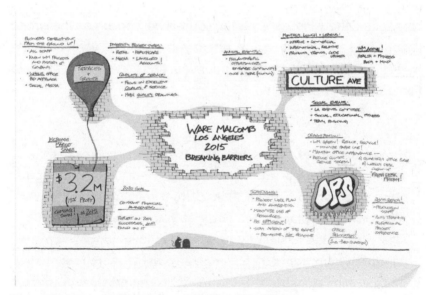

Example: Ware Malcomb Los Angeles Mind Map.

would be better at, Ken would take care of it and keep me informed of the outcome and any necessary actions. I had full confidence in his ability to handle any issues I asked him to take care of. Similarly, all our business leaders who run a business unit, office, or department also are encouraged to develop their #2. Having a Number Two is how you train your replacement. A leader cannot grow into the next big opportunity without a strong person to backfill their current role.

You must have that person in place once you get your team to a specific size. It's not the easiest thing. You have to either develop an employee who wants a challenge and wants more responsibility or hire somebody, bring them in, and mesh with them over time to build that level of trust. Either way, it takes time—and patience. You will go through trial and error to get the right fit where personalities and work styles mesh. But it's a discipline that you have to carry out. Otherwise, as a leader, you will be working on the wrong things. That's a road to failure where you either find yourself in the weeds, fall behind on strategic priorities, or hit a wall from exhaustion. Both are wrong turns.

> **Having a Number Two is how you train your replacement. A leader cannot grow into the next big opportunity without a strong person to backfill their current role. You must have that person in place once you get your team to a specific size. It's not the easiest thing. You have to either develop an employee who wants a challenge and wants more responsibility or hire somebody, bring them in, and mesh with them over time to build that level of trust. Either way, it takes time—and patience.**

You may be asking, is a Number Two another way of saying have a good senior aide-de-camp, a top assistant with aspirations?

Definitely! The Number Two goes beyond "task." Number Two is your partner reporting to you but offering a far greater span of reliance across roles and responsibilities.

The role changes depending on the day and what needs to be done in your office, company, or business. One day it might be solving an operational problem. Another might be solving a team org chart issue, a client issue that needs to be handled or assigned, or a marketing initiative that needs to be taken care of and developed. It's a great training ground for the person who is the Number Two. And often, that person in our company has been promoted to run a business themselves (such as Ken or Jay.)

Jay has proven to be an excellent architect during his tenure here. He has a deep understanding of the intricacies of the process and where our responsibilities lie. He is well versed in the technical aspects of specifications and can identify our liabilities.

When Jim and I initially hired Jay, we often assigned him to handle problematic projects. Jay approached these challenges in a systematic, rational, and logical manner. Unlike many individuals, he doesn't allow emotions to cloud his judgment when faced with project issues. Jay has a unique ability to step back and view problems objectively. He can accurately define where the responsibilities lie for our team, clients, and contractors. He has successfully managed to defuse numerous situations that could have escalated into more significant problems. We have affectionately dubbed him "The Mop Man" because of his talent for cleaning up messes.

"The Mop Man title was infamously bestowed on me many years ago because of my ability, and willingness, to take the lead on difficult dispute resolution issues with clients and industry partners by working through complex liability problems that can have significant financial exposure," Jay Todisco recounts.

"Many people tend to procrastinate or avoid dealing with issues of this nature that can be contentious and confrontational. I have learned that the uncomfortable aspects of this activity get magnified as these issues remain outstanding and drag on. I've learned the best course of action is to deal with these issues in a timely manner to facilitate the most expeditious means to the end. The client who is uncomfortable today will be contentious later."

A few pointers and prompts to keep in mind in developing your indispensable Number Two:

- If you have a candidate in mind, give them a couple of challenging assignments, check in regularly, but give enough space and wait for the results. Don't micromanage.
- Check in on workload and workflow to avoid overloading your Number Two.
- Schedule regular lunches or sit-downs to hear Number Two's feedback and suggestions.
- Your Number Two should have complementary strengths and weaknesses. You don't want your Number Two to be your clone! Cultivate candidates with strengths that offset your weaker skill sets.
- Look for these qualities: ambitious, creative, strong commitment to company culture and goals.
- See how they respond over time. Do they want this role?

Serving as Number Two is a great way to get on the Chessboard. In Ware Malcomb, Number Twos often earn their opportunity to open or take over an office.

The Chessboard

The Chessboard is a metaphor for employees on the management track available for different career moves in their and the company's interest. Jim and I shared a history of being on the Chessboard (before we thought of the metaphor): our leaders chose us to run new offices, prove ourselves, and then be promoted again. Jim came up with the name, and the Chessboard soon became an important strategic tool, plucking somebody out of an office or a department and giving them an opportunity to grow in their career. Sometimes it meant they had to

City Chess Set designed by Ted Heisler.

move across the country and open a new office, or maybe they were in an established office somewhere and we needed to move them to another office to take a leadership position. We move them around for the best advantage of the company and their career. It is always essential that it's an excellent opportunity for them to advance their career.

We have a lot of people who have been with us many years because they have been able to take advantage of these opportunities.

When you make an acquisition or bring in a senior person from outside, they have to embrace the culture and get used to a different culture and way of doing things, and we've done that. We have hired a lot of people in this way. We have made a few acquisitions, but the Chessboard is the preferred methodology and the logical progression from developing others and being aware of what they need to develop.

> **Jim came up with the name, and the Chessboard soon became an important strategic tool, plucking somebody out of an office or a department and giving them an opportunity to grow in their career. Sometimes it meant they had to move across the country and open a new office, or maybe they were in an established office somewhere and we needed to move them to another office to take a leadership position. We move them around for the best advantage of the company and their career.**

That's one reason why the baseline of our organic growth strategy is personal development and working together. Layers of leadership pulling in the same direction, staying connected, helping each other, and being integrated as one company honoring individual excellence: always stacking variations of leadership into a unified whole energized by personal opportunity and shared excellence.

It is the WM way.

Layering Personal and Financial Health

Growing up as a Midwest middle-class kid, I was taught the importance of being responsible and completing chores. While there was always plenty of time for fun and blowing off steam, maintaining a healthy balance was crucial. Unfortunately, my father's stressful job and health issues, which were not as well recognized then, took a toll on his well-being. He smoked. He had a heart attack when he was very young, at age 45. It traumatized the whole family. But it woke us up to health and taking care of ourselves. After open heart surgery and months of rehabilitation (medical technology since the 1970s has come a long way), he did a lot better. But we still lost him early at age 69, leaving a lasting impression on my brothers and me.

Ephemera. **Layered metal process.**

93

When I became a leader and faced the challenges of building a company during a recession, I found myself out of balance and struggling to maintain my health. It was a hard lesson, but I learned the importance of implementing balance and self-care incrementally over time.

Growing up in a middle-class household also taught me the importance of living within my means and saving money. My parents instilled in me the values of being conservative with spending and saving money whenever possible. These lessons have served me well throughout my life, and I am grateful for the financial stability they have provided.

In my work with United to End Homelessness, I learned how even one financial or health issue can lead to homelessness, despite a person's hard work and best efforts.

Maintaining balance in life is not limited to just family and health. All aspects of our lives, including relationships, finances, and professional experiences, contribute to a healthy ecosystem that supports us. When these layers are imbalanced, conflicts can arise. For instance, unexpected illnesses can disrupt our finances and divert our attention from work. Similarly, excessive stress and overwork can result in accidents and errors. As leaders and managers, it is crucial to consider all these dimensions and strive for sustained excellence. Strong relationships, finances, and health are the foundational pillars of success and happiness. We must also prioritize self-care and family to fully flourish. Regardless of our situation, we all encounter family concerns, making finding harmony in all aspects of our lives even more important.

As leaders and managers, it is crucial to consider all these dimensions and strive for sustained excellence. Strong relationships, finances, and health are the foundational pillars of success and happiness. We must also prioritize self-care and family to fully flourish. Regardless of our situation, we all encounter family concerns, making finding harmony in all aspects of our lives even more important.

Self-Care Paradox

Recently, a friend shared an article with me about how even doctors struggle with maintaining balance and how they can regain it. It was comforting to know that other professionals also fall into the trap of neglecting their personal lives while focusing on their work, but that there are commonsense solutions we can all implement.

According to John Schorling, MD, MPH, an internal medicine professor and director of physician wellness programs at the University of Virginia School of Medicine, finding balance requires effort, planning, and trade-offs. Schorling highlights a common phenomenon among physicians, where they tend to postpone their personal lives for the sake of their careers. He emphasizes that waiting for the future will not improve your life and recognizing that work/life balance requires proactive effort is the first step toward achieving it.

Schorling comments that the compulsive personality traits that got physicians into medical school and that make them good physicians are also contributors to a lack of balance in their lives. "Physicians get a lot of their self-worth from their work.

The importance that work has for physicians makes it hard for them to set priorities and recognize that other things are equally important."

Neglect of self-care, a compulsive drive to achieve, and the inability to prioritize are all traits that put physicians at risk for work-life imbalance. *If ignored, such imbalance can lead to grim consequences, including burnout, depression, divorce, behavioral problems, mood disorders, and substance abuse.*

Among his clients, Peter S. Moskowitz, MD, a life coach and the director of the Center for Professional and Personal Renewal, finds that people who burn out professionally are often those who had the brightest fires in the beginning. "Often the doctors who are the most compassionate, the most caring, and the hardest workers are the ones who get burned out," he says. They do not have a self-care program in place to sustain their energy, and they become depleted emotionally and spiritually.

To create a sustainable, balanced lifestyle, take time to objectively assess your physical and emotional wellness and then keep track of the key indicators of your well-being over time.[22]

I believe great doctors and leaders are built to last, which requires a balance and synthesis among life's layers of work, family, self-care, finances, and health. At Ware Malcomb, I wanted my team members and leaders to come to work unburdened by financial worries and practicing self-care.

Deferring Gratification

As Jay (our Mop Man and brilliant president) and I relaxed over a couple of beers one Friday afternoon in my office, talking about this book, Jay told me his dad used to say, "I don't mind spending money, but I hate wasting it." Jay shared with me how his father's advice provided financial security for their family and how he has tried to follow this concept throughout his life.

With his increasing responsibilities at Ware Malcomb, Jay's income also grew. Though he was tempted to splurge on a bigger house, a sports car, or a luxurious vacation, he knew it was essential to be practical and conservative with his finances. Thanks to the financial guidance provided by Ware Malcomb, Jay saved enough money to achieve his family's financial security goals through consistent and sensible strategies.

"I remember a few years back," Jay continued, "you mandated that every board of directors member produce a comprehensive personal financial statement, keep a close eye on their assets and liabilities, set measurable success goals, and share it with the rest of the board annually. That's not something I expected, and while I was surprised at first, it made sense.

"Why? The aim was twofold: first, to guarantee that each of us is on the path to financial stability for our families, and second, to ensure that the firm can navigate a recession, we must have the flexibility to temporarily suspend our salaries without risking our personal finances.

"Additionally, there are future considerations, right? When a partner retires and begins their buyout process, the remaining partners' financial position won't burden others or hinder their ability to buy out the other. This oversight and advice created a sense of accountability that wouldn't exist otherwise, as I knew the board would monitor my wealth generation progress and report it back to my partners."

"And now?" I asked him.

Jay laughed, saying, "It took many years of living within my budget and sticking to a conservative spending plan, but I finally achieved true financial stability. Now I can treat myself to the sleek Italian convertible I've dreamed of for so long."

Open Books Protocol for Leaders

Over time, as CEO, I realized that it's also important for all of our leaders to be financially responsible and not overspend. This ensures that their personal financial situation doesn't become a distraction from their leadership responsibilities. For example, the commercial real estate sector is one of the first to experience a slump when economic indicators turn negative. So when Ware Malcomb hits a downturn (and, undoubtedly, many companies have similar practices), we start with asking leaders for sacrifices. The board shuts off their salary for an agreed-upon period. Before we are forced to lay anyone off, that's where we start.

> **Over time, as CEO, I realized that it's also important for all of our leaders to be financially responsible and not overspend. This ensures that their personal financial situation doesn't become a distraction from their leadership responsibilities.**

This policy emphasizes the importance of having financially strong top executives. At the board level, we have established clear financial planning protocols to ensure that those overseeing the company's well-being are not financially burdened and can focus on growth. Regular reviews of board members' finances at Ware Malcomb help to implement these measures and provide leaders with the resources they need to invest in the company's future.

Discussing employees' personal lives may seem unusual or controversial, and we have safeguards in place. All disclosures and participation are voluntary. We want our leadership team to be strong because if you are not financially strong, you will be distracted at work and unable to do your job as well due to worry. We don't want you to be in that situation.

To help all of our leaders, I wrote two manifestos that outline my personal methods for accumulating wealth and maintaining good health. While these methods may not be groundbreaking, they have been effective for me, and I hope they can help others too. Without good health and financial stability, it's difficult to be successful. These are crucial layers to achieving success, and whatever your personal approach is, they cannot be ignored. Financial health provides stability and strength for all your family's endeavors and goals. Good health provides the font of energy your life requires.

I share my examples to inspire others and reinforce the importance of these layers.

Finance: The Stabilizing Layer

Over the years, many leaders have asked me to share my thoughts on personal financial management. It is a crucial discipline, regardless of age or income level. I share my method because it has proven effective for me, and I firmly believe that a disciplined approach is essential for achieving long-term financial security.

Here are some steps you can take to manage your finances effectively:

- Create a personal financial statement and update it every quarter. This will give you a clear idea of your current financial standing and help you plan for the future. Should you have a significant other, set up a process to coordinate and find consensus.

- Make a monthly budget that includes your income, fixed expenses, variable expenses, savings, and contingencies. Keep updating it as your circumstances change. Whether you're saving up for a major purchase, paying off debt, or simply trying to stay on top of your finances, a well-planned budget can provide the structure and guidance you need to stay focused and successful. So take the time to create a budget that works for you, and commit to reviewing and updating it regularly. Your financial future will thank you!

- Make sure your mortgage or rent payment does not exceed 28% of your gross salary, and avoid interest-only mortgages.

- Develop a habit of saving regularly and open an investment account to save a certain percentage (10–20%) of your income. Don't use this money; let it grow.

- If you receive an incentive or performance bonus, save most of it and only spend a small portion (10–20%). Allow the saved amount to accumulate over time.

- Maximize your IRAs and 401(k)s every year and don't touch the money saved.

- If you have dependents, get life and disability insurance. Both are important to protect your family's financial security if the unthinkable happens.

- Get an umbrella insurance policy. Umbrella insurance, also known as personal excess liability insurance, is normally very affordable and provides additional coverage beyond the limits of your primary insurance policies, such as home or auto insurance.

- Buy cars that you can own and maintain even after the loan pays off. Keep them long term; don't flip every two to three years. New cars tend to experience significant depreciation in the first few years. By holding on to your car, you avoid the steepest depreciation, saving you money in the long run. You eliminate monthly car payments once you've paid off your car loan. This can free up a significant portion of your budget for other financial goals or expenses. As a car ages, its value decreases, leading to lower insurance premiums.

- Keep two credit cards: one with flight miles and another as a backup. Avoid gas and department store cards and pay the bills off every month to avoid interest charges.

- Set up a revocable trust. A revocable trust is a legal arrangement where a person transfers ownership of their assets into a trust during their lifetime. This trust offers several benefits, including avoiding probate, maintaining privacy, planning for incapacity, and providing flexibility and control for the grantor.

It's essential to remember that building wealth requires discipline, commitment, and dedication, just like any other pursuit in life. You and your colleagues undoubtedly put in a lot of hard work, do an exceptional job, and achieve impressive results. Ensure that your team directs the same level of effort toward securing long-term financial stability.

Health: The Energy Layer

My health manifesto outlines the strategies I've found most helpful in maintaining balance and avoiding burnout. As a wellness advocate, I believe establishing a layered approach to self-care is essential for achieving physical and mental balance. It all starts with building a strong foundation for wellness. Once you have established a solid foundation, you can build upon it with other habits that align with your interests and fitness level.

One example of a beneficial habit to incorporate is practicing tai chi, a Chinese martial art that focuses on balance, strength, flexibility, and inner calm. Other habits contributing to overall wellness include getting good sleep, meditating, and cooking healthy meals. I practice Pilates as well as strength training, and I find skiing and golf to be great ways to stay fit year-round and keep my mind and body in balance. I struggled for years to establish a consistent workout routine. My attempts to work out during lunchtime were always derailed by work needs.

Sandy encouraged me to schedule one Pilates session per week. I succeeded in committing to a regular appointment and added another Pilates session. I hired a personal trainer for twice-weekly strength training and fast-walk twice a week.

Work can be overwhelming, but take the long view, the whole-brain approach, and make time for your interests and passions. Music has always been very important to me, as I am a big music lover. Although I used to play guitar, it didn't become one of my primary pursuits, but I still enjoy it. The process of synthesizing different ideas to create a beautiful piece of art is what fascinates me about music. It's like a band writing a song or an album where they take various ideas from different people and turn them into sounds and melodies. They use different instruments and vocals to create harmonies and put it all together to make a beautiful piece of art. I see a direct relationship between this process and the synthesis of different ideas that I'm talking about in this book.

When listening to a song, I love to try to isolate the different instruments and how they layer in to create a whole. It's fascinating to me and serves as inspiration, maybe a metaphor for what I'm trying to do with layered leadership. A great example happened at George Harrison's tribute ceremony at the Rock & Roll Hall of Fame induction ceremony in Cleveland. Prince played an incredible guitar solo during the All-Star performance of "While My Guitar Gently Weeps." It was awesome. He creatively layered that solo on an already existing epic.

FLR 1.15 ORA (48" x 48"). **Mixed media.**

Music is an incredible thing. I recall a time when Jim and I were hanging out one afternoon at a bar in Park City. A Led Zeppelin song started playing. Initially, I was half dozing off in the sun as the song was playing, but suddenly I got into it. I was really feeling the layers in the music, lost in my own thoughts. Jim noticed how I was reacting and said, "You were really into that; it must be important to you." I agreed and explained that music is super important to me and that I've learned a lot from it.

In line with Vince Lombardi's philosophy, I believe that true leaders are made, not born. And to become a successful leader, it is crucial to prioritize self-care. I consider self-care to be an attitude, a mindset, and a way of life that requires training, effort, and a commitment to oneself.

To achieve this, I recommend adopting one change at a time. Start with the easiest habit to incorporate, and gradually build on it. The key is to be committed to yourself and take pride in incremental progress. Everyone faces unique challenges that call for customized solutions that cater to their family's requirements.

As a leader, it's important to prioritize your own well-being. You are a trusted and valuable member of the team, and taking care of yourself is essential for your long-term success, health, and happiness. Self-care requires effort, commitment, and training, but it's worth it in the end. The suggestions below may seem basic and obvious, but they have worked for me over time. Remember, this is an incremental process. Start by adopting one change at a time, beginning with the easiest. Eliminate or reduce one bad habit and replace it with a good one. Take pride in your incremental progress and commit to yourself.

Self-Care: The Balancing Layer

Here are nine tips for a healthier lifestyle that you can incorporate into your routine. Again, I'm no expert, and there are tons of books written about this stuff, but these ideas have worked for me:

- Make one permanent change to your diet at a time and build on it. If you're looking to make changes to your diet, it's important to take things one step at a time. This approach can help make the transition to a healthier diet feel less overwhelming and more manageable. Remember, small changes can often lead to big results in the long run.

- Consider taking vitamins and supplements daily depending upon your personal situation, such as diet. It can be a good idea to consider taking vitamins regularly as they can benefit your overall health. However, before starting any new vitamin regimen, it is important to consult with your doctor to determine which specific vitamins are right for you based on your individual needs and health status.

- Stay hydrated throughout the day. It is highly recommended that you drink an adequate amount of water to stay hydrated and maintain good health. Dehydration can cause several health issues, such as headaches, fatigue, and dizziness. Therefore, make sure you consume enough fluids and keep yourself hydrated.

- Getting enough quality sleep is crucial for maintaining good health and well-being. While it's generally recommended that adults aim for seven to eight hours of sleep each night, finding the amount of sleep that works best for you is important. Everyone has different sleep needs based on their body and lifestyle. Make sure to prioritize a consistent sleep pattern in your daily routine to ensure you wake up feeling well rested and ready to tackle the day.

- Find an exercise routine that you enjoy and commit to it on a regular basis. Start small and gradually increase as you become more comfortable. Finding an exercise routine that you enjoy will help you stay motivated and make the experience more sustainable. Consistency is vital when it comes to achieving long-term fitness success.

- Spending time in nature can help clear your mind and spark creativity. Whether it's a stroll through a local park or a hike in the mountains, spending time in nature can be a wonderful way to unwind, de-stress, and reconnect with the world around us.

- It's important to prioritize self-care, and one effective way to do so is by getting regular massages. This practice helps with physical relaxation and tension relief, improves mental well-being, and can enhance one's overall quality of life.

- Don't skip regular doctor appointments, including a yearly physical, dentist visit, eye doctor checkup, and any recommended screenings.

- Share your challenges with someone you trust and take things one step at a time. Remember that new habits take time and commitment to develop. It can be tough to face challenges alone, so it's always a good idea to confide in someone you trust. Developing new habits requires both time and commitment, so be kind to yourself and take it at your own pace.

Work/Life Balance

- To effectively delegate tasks, it is important to hold people accountable and avoid doing their job for them. It is crucial to identify your Number Two and make it a priority if you do not have one already.

- Avoid being a helicopter manager or micromanager and empower your team by showing them that you trust them. Doing so will encourage your team to take ownership of their work, boost their morale, and foster a more positive work environment. So resist the urge to micromanage and embrace a leadership style that empowers your team to shine. This will help you stay focused on your own work without overloading yourself.

- It is important to guard against overworking yourself and becoming a workaholic. Identify a trusted person who can help keep you accountable and support you. This person could be a friend, colleague, mentor, or even a professional coach who can offer guidance and help you establish healthy boundaries to prevent burnout. Asking for help is a sign of strength, not weakness.

- Take a break from your technology and avoid sending digital communication outside of normal business hours. Sending emails late at night is not impressive to anyone and can actually be harmful to you over the long run.

- Commit to a schedule:
    - For work hours.
    - For exercise.
    - For family time.
    - For screen-free time.

- Be efficient:
    - When making decisions.
    - By striving not to revisit issues more than once.
    - By cleaning out your inbox (defeat the tyranny of email!).

- Schedule vacations and take them:
    - No emailing on vacation.
    - No calls on vacation.
    - Set expectations before you go.
    - Use the time off as a chance to empower and test your people.

Attitude

- Avoid beating yourself up about any of these issues:

  - It's a journey.

  - Stay positive.

- Adopt an optimistic attitude. Optimists tend to be healthier and happier—and win!

- You are setting the example for your team. This is very important. Your attitude affects them, for good or bad.

- Feel good about yourself and all you have accomplished. You are awesome!

- Adopt an attitude of gratitude. In essence, this means actively focusing on the positive aspects of our lives and being thankful for them. By doing so, we can cultivate a sense of contentment and fulfillment, which can help us to better cope with challenges and setbacks. Adopting an attitude of gratitude can also improve our relationships with others, as it encourages us to be more empathetic and kind. So whether it's through writing in a gratitude journal or simply taking a moment to reflect on the things we're thankful for, incorporating gratitude into our daily lives can have a profoundly positive impact.

- Adopt an attitude of continuous improvement. Deciding to make a change may seem simple, but the real challenge lies in following through and maintaining consistency. This is what sets successful individuals apart from those who remain stagnant. Remember, you are solely responsible for your actions and choices. As Angel Cipolla, my fitness trainer, wisely said, "It. Is. 100%. Up. To. You."

Part Two

Develop a Vision, Build a Plan

5

Strategy by Design:
The Planning Layer

"If you can't describe your strategy in twenty minutes, simply and in plain language, you haven't got a plan."

—Lawrence Bossidy and Ram Charan

As a leader, whether you hold the position of a CEO or manage a small business unit, it is crucial to maintain a forward-thinking mindset. Your attention should be directed toward your vision of where your company is headed, how you want to get there, and how to consistently achieve the goals that you set. Committing your vision to writing and outlining your company's potential will make a significant difference. It establishes a structure for accomplishing daily tasks, achieving yearly objectives, and even planning for the next five years.

Therefore, your business plan should align with this vision and serve as a road map toward your goals. It is important to note that falling short of your goals in one year can make it difficult to catch up in the next. This is why it's critical to constantly evaluate your progress, make necessary adjustments, and remain committed to your vision. A well-crafted business plan should never be filed away and forgotten. It should be a living, breathing document that is continually updated with progress as well as setbacks and used to guide your decision-making process. So take the time to develop a clear and concise business plan that aligns with your vision, and you'll be well on your way to achieving your goals.

Whether a creative services, professional services, legal, or medical firm, *run a great business, not simply a great services firm.* Develop strategies and goals, and then execute them. This is how you will outdistance your competitors. *Accountable* is described by Webster's as containing the meanings "answerable," "responsible," and "explainable." In running a business, executing against strategy in this way means doing all three: explaining one's decisions, answering to them, and being responsible for them. That's the beauty of it. *Accountability* is a term that is commonly used, but this process is what delivers results and benefits.

The Elements of Process Execution

Strategic planning can be overwhelming, with plenty of terminology and complex processes. I want to offer you a simple, easy-to-understand process for creating actionable plans for your business, unit, or team.

Lawrence Bossidy and Ram Charan changed business history with their book *Execution.* They wrote, "If you can't describe your strategy in twenty minutes, simply and in plain language, you haven't got a plan. 'But,' people may say, 'I've got a complex strategy. It can't be reduced to a page.' That's nonsense. That's not a complex strategy. It's a complex thought about the strategy."

You can learn research methods to identify pathways to success based on your organization and sector. One effective approach is to analyze both successful and failed businesses to determine the factors that contributed to their outcomes. This information can then be used to inform your strategic vision. For example, consider our comparison of Home Depot's success to the failed HomeClub. Both had similar business goals and were founded within five years of each other.

Marana (20" x 29"). Limited-edition print.

Throughout the strategic planning process, start and end with the guiding principle used by successful companies like Toyota, Costco, Ritz-Carlton, and Ware Malcomb: always connecting and always helping.

Throughout the strategic planning process, start and end with the guiding principle used by successful companies like Toyota, Costco, Ritz-Carlton, and Ware Malcomb: always connecting and always helping.

Fleet of Ships

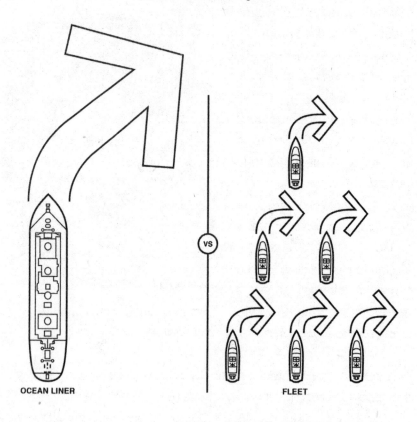

OCEAN LINER

VS

FLEET

You can foster a culture that stays nimble as you grow when your leaders are able to move together in formation. As previewed earlier, I launched the fleet of ships metaphor at one of the leadership meetings as an opportunity for leaders to improve communication and alignment. The metaphor effectively captures how to share information, identify objectives, align priorities, work together toward a shared vision and mission, and shift quickly in unison when necessary.

There is no process execution without close coordination. Our regional leaders and the executive team have developed a seamless way of operating over the years. They share insights and strategies that help them respond and change direction effectively. I have observed that many giants in our industry have a slow-moving approach, like that of an ocean liner. On the other hand, our team is like a fleet of smaller vessels that can move quickly and make course corrections when needed without losing speed. Staying connected as a company is vital for strategy coordination so we can help each other out. When we create our strategic plans, we ensure that they are comprehensive and include specific steps that we will take to achieve our goals.

The specifics of each plan may differ depending on the market and the size of the office. For example, when we enter a new market, our priority is to attract new customers to our primary business and create long-lasting connections with them. This may involve focusing on national players with whom we already have established relationships in other markets, as well as local clients who are important to us. We take proactive measures to reach out to these clients, including attending events and networking opportunities.

I have observed that many giants in our industry have a slow-moving approach, like that of an ocean liner. On the other hand, our team is like a fleet of smaller vessels that can move quickly and make course corrections when needed without losing speed. Staying connected as a company is vital for strategy coordination so we can help each other out. When we create our strategic plans, we ensure that they are comprehensive and include specific steps that we will take to achieve our goals.

We aim to create opportunities that demonstrate our capabilities in order to secure their business. We also focus on where the market's strengths align with our own, whether it is the industrial sector, interiors, or corporate accounts.

Accountability

As business leaders, we are held accountable for our progress toward our goals. We report on our progress at our regular business meetings, which allows for consistent check-ins and ensures that we are making meaningful progress toward our objectives. This level of accountability and discipline drives us to take action and make progress every day, as we know that we will be reporting on our progress at our next meeting. Our strategic plans are scrutinized to ensure they are ambitious yet realistic and achievable, with the ultimate goal of driving growth and success for our business.

Change Fast

Encourage a culture of adaptability and agility to respond to changes in the market and business environment. As a team, we can pivot our direction quickly if we all decide to do so. To ensure this, we make a conscious effort to meet often and stay connected as a company. We use the leadership meetings to discuss changes, gather ideas, and issue new directions for our fleet of ships. This is an essential aspect of our work culture, where we help and support each other during economic events or global disruptions like the COVID-19 pandemic, for example, when we saw our business grow. Our leadership team has instilled this attitude across our firm, that we are all in this together and desire to help all our office leaders succeed with their plans.

> Encourage a culture of adaptability and agility to respond to changes in the market and business environment.

Always Helping

However, we understand that struggles are a part of the journey, and when our colleagues face roadblocks, we strategize around them and find a way forward. This approach has proven effective, and we have seen positive outcomes. We believe that this one-team attitude, where we stay connected and help each other, sets us apart.

We aspire not to work in silos and believe that success is both an individual and team achievement. As a result, we are always connecting the dots for our national clients, ensuring that we're always in motion and consistently making progress. Our work is not about dictating from the ivory tower; it's about staying connected and helping each other to achieve our goals.

Now we will look at what makes our process work, so we understand, gain, and protect our competitive advantage.

1. Determine Your Competitive Advantage

To achieve a dominant market share, it is essential to understand and define your target market. Ware Malcomb is the leading industrial and commercial real estate design firm. We learned that when contemplating expanding into a new market, the first step is to focus on your core customers and build out from there.

Ware Malcomb strategically chooses office locations based on our market research, including locations where our best customers have a presence. We survey our competition and find opportunities to fill gaps in the market. Building relationships is crucial for success. Attending professional real estate organizations is also essential. As we staff a new office, we have a ramp-up routine from interviewing engaging community leaders to making new hires. We have executed this process multiple times and are continuously improving it.

Selecting the right local office leader is paramount and forms the first layer of strategy. This can be achieved by identifying the right person within the organization (Chessboard) or choosing the best candidate available in the market through a thorough interview process. When an external candidate is selected, a supporting member of the WM team will be assigned to assist the new leader in understanding the company culture and navigating the organization toward success.

Carefully diversifying beyond our core market is critical to sustaining competitive strength. In the early '90s, our company experienced a downturn as a result of a major commercial real estate slump, as we were less diverse in terms of the type of work we did, mostly catering to industrial and office developers. However, we *had* added interior design to our services in a smaller capacity, which my office in Woodland Hills mainly handled.

It was a scary period. I was young, untested, and barely passing the stress test of that time. I probably had days when it felt like I had the highest cortisol load of anyone in architecture. Here's what helped. During that time, my partner Jim and I had to have serious conversations about the future of the company: how we could strengthen it, the type of people we needed, the work we wanted to do, and our vision and values. We sat down and defined all of this in detail, realizing the importance of writing it all down and committing to it. Bill and Bill were instrumental in helping us figure things out. They set a great example of a partnership with a similar philosophy about their company, and we aimed to follow suit.

Jim and I had not known each other before working for the company, but Bill and Bill threw us together to handle the company's transition. We became equal partners, with me as CEO and Jim as president. We discussed everything and worked out any disagreements to decide on the direction for the company. Our partnership was built on mutual trust, respect, and creativity, with each of us bringing our ideas and experience to the table. We eventually became great friends and business partners, and our relationship was crucial to the company's success. Identifying our diversification approach was a company-saving outcome of our partnership.

During that time, we focused on expanding and improving our interiors business line within our firm. Initially, hiring people and pursuing this type of work was challenging because we weren't well known for it. However, we persevered, and now we have one of the largest interior practices in the country, representing 30–35% of our business.

As a leader, it's crucial to develop a clear vision for your market and how your company can improve its understanding, growth, and protection.

Thinking Against the Grain: A Contrarian Layer

At Ware Malcomb, we continuously strive to learn and develop how to best serve our clients on our terms and through standards that mesh with our culture. Although we work in a profession that has been around for centuries, we don't just do what our industry or competitors do.

One book that has inspired us is *Freakonomics*, which debunks conventional wisdom and encourages thinking for ourselves. We aim to avoid groupthink and focus instead on what's best for our company and clients. This mindset has helped us tremendously to know and invest in our competitive strengths.

We developed a flag with arrows pointing in one direction, except for one arrow (representing WM) that goes the opposite way. This symbolizes our rebellious approach to constantly rethinking and adapting. All our offices use it to encourage independent thinking, creativity, and challenging the status quo.

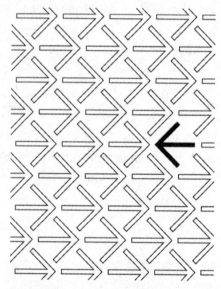

Sometimes making tough decisions is necessary, but it's not just about people. It's also about being quick to adapt to current and future needs. Kodak's inability to respond quickly to the advent of digital photography is an example of this.

Another aspect of being a smart contrarian: avoid imitating other competitors or expanding into markets where **WM developed a flag that symbolizes our approach to tune out the noise and encourage independent thinking, creativity, and challenging the status quo.**

you lack historical expertise. For instance, JCPenney and Radio-Shack both attempted to expand into new markets but lost sight of their core business models and consequently suffered declining sales.

Home Depot vs. HomeClub: The Research Layer

A useful approach to obtain knowledge about your market and the elements that influence the success or failure of related businesses is to carry out a de-layering analysis. This involves closely examining and comparing two similar competing companies, such as Home Depot and the now defunct HomeClub, which were established around the same time and shared comparable business objectives. By analyzing the differences in their approaches and outcomes, you can better understand the factors that lead to success or failure in their industry.

The reason we conduct these studies is twofold: First, WM is not the first company to attempt visionary growth and experience the challenges that go along with it. We can learn from other businesses that came before our time. Second, our approach to studying companies outside of our industry reinforces our culture to be a great business, not just a great design firm. This is a critical strategic layer of WM.

Home Depot and HomeClub were both home improvement retailers that operated during the same period in the late 1990s. Home Depot succeeded, while HomeClub eventually failed and filed for bankruptcy in 2001. Along the way, HomeClub changed its name to HomeBase. Then, it liquidated its first network of stores to attempt

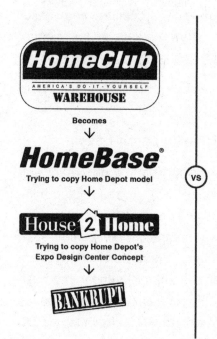

Becomes
↓

Trying to copy Home Depot model

↓

Trying to copy Home Depot's
Expo Design Center Concept

↓

MARKET LEADER
FORTUNE 500 Company

> **BUSINESS/LEADERSHIP LESSON:**
> It is important that we understand our unique mission, values and who we are as a company.
> If we always follow the competition, we will lose.

HomeClub vs. Home Depot.

to survive as a new House2Home chain with more furnishings, linens, and appliances (akin to Bed Bath & Beyond), which also shortly went out of business.

"HomeBase Inc., caving in to home-improvement giants Home Depot Inc. and Lowe's Cos., said Tuesday that it will bail out of the home-improvement sector entirely, closing 22 stores and converting 62 others into home furnishings businesses," the *Los Angeles Times* reported in December 2000.[23]

> The Irvine company will stake its future on its House2Home stores, noting that five of these test home furnishing sites generated strong sales in their first 12 weeks.

The company closed 31 HomeBase stores Tuesday—most of them in Southern California—and plans to shut down the remaining HomeBase stores in stages over the next few months. The stores will reopen by Friday for liquidation sales.

The stores being converted to the House2Home concept are expected to reopen in the new format over the coming year. In Orange County, HomeBase will convert stores in Brea, Stanton, Irvine, Santa Ana and Laguna Niguel into House2Home sites.

House2Home went bankrupt within the year as well.

A huge differentiator for Home Depot was its customer-centric business model. Home Depot focuses on providing a wide selection of products, competitive prices, and excellent customer service to cater to do-it-yourself (DIY) customers. Home Depot organized the value proposition around the customer. The stores were designed to be a one-stop shop for all home improvement needs, offering a seamless and convenient shopping experience. HomeClub, on the other hand, struggled to differentiate itself from competitors and failed to establish a unique value proposition, leading to a less compelling business model. Home Depot helped teach us the advantages of building a seamless and all-of-the-above service suite in industrial and commercial real estate, particularly with national clients.

Another factor that contributed to Home Depot's success was its strong branding and reputation. Home Depot invested heavily in branding and marketing to establish itself as a trusted and recognizable brand in the home improvement industry. Its strong reputation for quality products and helpful staff helped build customer loyalty and trust. HomeClub, on the other hand, failed to build a strong brand identity and did not resonate as effectively with consumers.

Home Depot's success was partly due to its focus on new home-owners, DIY homeowners, contractors, builders, and others involved in home improvement, renovation, and repair. The company caters to diverse customers and selects store locations based on new and growing residential and real estate construction.

Home Depot expanded aggressively, strategically locating stores in high-traffic areas. In contrast, HomeClub had slower expansion, struggled with prime locations, and had lower visibility. Also, Home Depot's success can be attributed to its strong financial management, allowing it to weather economic downturns and invest in growth. Meanwhile, HomeClub's financial challenges and debt burdens hindered its ability to expand and improve.

Leadership and a robust defining identity are critical factors in a company's success. Home Depot's teams had a strong vision and executed well, staying ahead of the competition by responding to market changes and customer demands. HomeClub suffered from leadership and management issues, causing strategic missteps and inefficiencies.

Home Depot offers not just products and services but solutions too. This is also the approach Ware Malcomb takes with our clients. Knowing who you are, sticking to your guns, and building on your strengths is a huge lesson we took from the strategy.

Coke vs. Pepsi: Research Layer 2

Despite operating in the same industry and offering similar products, PepsiCo and the Coca-Cola Company, also known as Pepsi and Coke, have unique strategic plans that set them apart and lead to success. This shows that understanding one's market and competition can lead to different pathways to success.

Coca-Cola positions itself in the concentrate business, not the cola business, while PepsiCo positions itself in the snack and beverage industry. PepsiCo has implemented a significant diversification and acquisition strategy to expand its business. Over the years, the company has made several acquisitions that have helped it grow and increase its market share. One of the most notable acquisitions was its merger with Lay's in 1965, which led to the creation of PepsiCo.

PepsiCo also had a successful business model with fast-food chains, having bought Yum! Brands, which included popular restaurants like KFC, Taco Bell, and Pizza Hut. In 1997, PepsiCo separated Yum! Brands into a separate publicly traded company. Additionally, PepsiCo once owned California Pizza Kitchen (CPK), a casual dining chain famous for its creative pizza options, and later sold it.

PepsiCo acquired Tropicana in 1998 and Quaker Oats in 2001. These acquisitions have played a crucial role in PepsiCo's growth and success, allowing it to offer its customers a wide range of products.

Coca-Cola's main strategy for achieving profit and growth is to dominate a market segment entirely by using exclusivity contracts to limit competition. Additionally, they purchase existing brands that complement Coke and even those that compete with Pepsi. Coca-Cola owns some bottlers and distributors but is far from owning a majority. Through vertical integration, Coca-Cola drives value by owning or controlling distribution and bottling.

The beverage titan drives profits through sales of concentrates and syrups:

> The Coca-Cola Company does not own, manage or control most local bottling companies.

> In our concentrate operations, The Coca-Cola Company typically generates net operating revenues by selling concentrates and syrups to authorized bottling partners.

> Our bottling partners combine the concentrates with still and/or sparkling water, and/or sweeteners, depending on the product, to prepare, package, sell and distribute finished beverages.

> Our finished product operations consist primarily of company-owned or -controlled bottling, sales and distribution operations.[24]

PepsiCo targets youthful consumers with lifestyle branding, while Coca-Cola emphasizes its classic image. Pepsi uses edgy marketing with celebrity endorsements, while Coca-Cola focuses on emotional advertising. Both have global distribution networks but differ in strategic plans and research priorities.

The two beverage giants also instill and reward shared values and commitment to the customer within their culture. Both companies represent excellent examples of defining their identity and executing on their vision, even though they choose different approaches to their competitive landscape.

2. Pursue Your Competitive Advantage

Once you have rigorously identified and communicated the heart of the market where you want to succeed, then you pursue your competitive advantage and eliminate competition. One way to do this is to swim to blue oceans—that is, to find untapped markets or niches that aren't already saturated with competitors. Another key strategy is to leverage client relationships, building trust and loyalty with your customers to keep them coming back for more.

Swim to Blue Oceans

Ware Malcomb owes a great debt to the work of W. Chan Kim and Renée Mauborgne in their book *Blue Ocean Strategy: How to Create Uncontested Market Space and Make the Competition Irrelevant*. This strategy focuses on creating new market space or "blue oceans" where companies can operate without facing direct competition, as opposed to competing in existing markets or "red oceans," where competition is intense and commoditized. We have adapted the strategy to our firm and markets, and I urge you to do the same.

The concept of red oceans refers to industries that are currently established and competitive, while blue oceans refer to untapped market opportunities that have yet to be explored. Understanding the difference between these two types of markets is integral to strategic planning and business development.

When it comes to blue oceans, traditional competition is not a factor. This is because the rules of the game have yet to be established. The concept of Blue Ocean Strategy involves reconstructing market boundaries to break away from typical competition. A business can create a unique identity and a compelling tagline by focusing on the big picture and producing a strategic plan that diverges from the competition. Additionally, it is essential to reach beyond existing clients and actively seek out nonclients. To successfully implement this strategy, it is essential to get the sequence right. This means considering how to create a winning opportunity for clients first, and then for oneself. By following these principles, a business can successfully navigate the blue ocean and establish itself as a leader in its industry.

In our industry, leveraging client relationships, or LCR, is an excellent way to tap into a blue ocean. As a company, we deploy LCR to transfer a client relationship from one part of the company to another, with the ideal outcome being that all offices in the organization will be working with this client. This approach may seem simple, but it requires a One Team attitude, culture, and focused hard work to make it a reality.

> **In our industry, leveraging client relationships, or LCR, is an excellent way to tap into a blue ocean. As a company, we deploy LCR to transfer a client relationship from one part of the company to another, with the ideal outcome being that all offices in the organization will be working with this client.**

For instance, let's say we have a client from Denver. We know that they have an office in Chicago, but we're not doing business with them in that location yet. In this situation, the two offices will collaborate to get the necessary introductions and hopefully leverage the relationship with the client. This could result in an endorsement from the client office in Denver to the Chicago office.

LCR is a specific strategy that we employ to ensure that we're taking full advantage of our client relationships and leveraging them for the benefit of the client and the organization.

One of our recent ideas was to add building measurement services to our company, which is a bit of a blue ocean for us because our big clients need this service. We strive to make the process seamless for them so they don't have to find a smaller specialty firm to do this work. This is another example of how we diversify carefully within our range of expertise, which tends to be more high level and then implemented specifically across the platform.

However, we don't try implementing the same strategies in all markets. Different markets have different market opportunities. For example, we may strategize differently in New York City than we do in Phoenix, which is an important industrial market, while New York offers more high-end interiors work. So, in each case, we may initially focus on the blue ocean that market may offer to us, and then we build the rest of the product and service offerings around them as we grow, and try to be consistent about it.

There's always room for growth, but it doesn't happen automatically. You must work at it and strategize. For example, we are in several science- and technology-oriented regions (San Diego, Seattle, and Washington, DC, for example), and we must provide expertise and staff to address regional trends that may not exist in other offices. Therefore, we target the market trend in that region or city and build diversification around it. Whether you're in a big or small office, there's always diversification to add, and you'll never run out of opportunities to keep building market share that's in line with your vision.

Execution

According to Lawrence Bossidy, execution exposes reality in a systematic way, and it is the heart of success. Successful companies achieve competitive advantage by facing reality, tracking progress against goals, and understanding the factors that lead to success or disappointment. Executing a strategy involves aligning people with goals and achieving results. Unfortunately, many organizations are full of people who try to avoid or shade reality, therefore eroding trust and cooperation throughout the firm.

Architecture firms have a long-standing reputation for not being great businesses. We were never going to succumb to that. We wanted to be both a great firm and a great business. So that's been super important to us because you can't do all this stuff we're trying to do if you're not a good business—you just can't do it. Have we made mistakes? Uh, tons! Our hiring process was a revolving door in my early years as CEO because we didn't have a refined recruiting and assessment process. Hires could have sterling technical skills and steal the show with their creativity and designs but fail at training and development and/or our cultural practices of always connecting and always helping.

Whatever your business is, strive for execution and performance. I know Ware Malcomb succeeded because the discipline of our systems and process execution created our blue ocean and our strategy.

All of these elements integrate to form our blue ocean against our competition. In many ways, other firms can't compete. Forgive me for saying this, but they can't touch us. And that's what you want.

3. Protect Your Competitive Advantage

As you strive to dominate a particular niche, insist on consistency, quality, and responsiveness to clients. You've sharpened your edge; now you need systems to hone it. Operations, admin, and design team members form the point of the spear in maintaining these aspects.

Leaders must regularly check in with their team to ensure everyone is on the same page. Respond promptly to any opportunities or concerns from clients to maintain their trust and loyalty. Hit your marks; make your deadlines.

The process of designing for commercial real estate development is continuous. It starts with creating a competitive proposal, followed by fast and quality deliverables. Problems may arise along the way, but addressing them promptly and working together to find solutions is important. Relationships with clients, consultants, contractors, and local building departments are essential for success.

When we're invited to propose on a project, we ensure that our fees are competitive with the industry. This is particularly important in commercial real estate, where everything, including our fees, is derived from the rent formula and cap rate. Our goal is to create a building that can charge rent based on market dictates. Therefore, everyone involved in the process must fit into this formula. Speed to market is crucial in commercial real estate development as it kick-starts the cash flow to our clients. Hence, we have developed systems in our company that allow us to be fast without compromising on quality. Quality is of utmost importance to us.

Road Runner and the Coyote—Layering Business Development and Operations

Layering business development and operations must be done in balance. If your hard-charging business development executives outrun the operational folks, client work may suffer. To illustrate the concept to our leaders, I turned to one of my favorite childhood cartoons and called it the Road Runner and the Coyote. Business development is the Road Runner; operations is the Coyote. The Coyote can never catch the Road Runner, but he must never be too far behind. Otherwise, your operational wheels fall off, and your performance drops.

GETTY/PICTURELAKE.

It's an eternal battle of need versus speed, aggravation versus acceleration. The luckless Coyote comes up with increasingly elaborate and seemingly foolproof schemes to snag the Road Runner, who, oblivious to the danger, always eludes the pathetic Coyote's painstaking plans. The metaphor is now part of WM's culture, a memorable concept for how we manage the active layer between growth and execution. In our metaphor, the Road Runner can't be leading the Coyote off the cliff where he hangs in midair until he looks down, and *bam!* The Road Runner may be faster, but she's sharing navigational information with the Coyote. Heck, sometimes we let the Coyote catch up.

Let's take a look at drawing production, a critical operation.

Our drawing production process is streamlined, and we have implemented measures to maintain quality control. Project managers are the backbone of our customer service team and are always ready to address any issues that may arise. Although we strive for perfection, we understand that issues can arise occasionally. For example, sometimes consultants may not coordinate their drawings properly, or our project teams may overlook a particular detail. In such cases, we believe that timely and efficient problem-solving is key. We encourage our team members to face challenges head-on and to tackle them as soon as they arise. We believe that delaying a response only exacerbates the issue. Hence, we have trained our team members to be proactive and address any problems that may arise immediately.

The Mop Man is our procrastination slayer and role model: "Dealing with contentious and confrontational issues is something that people often procrastinate or avoid altogether. As someone who has experienced the discomfort of leaving these issues unaddressed," Jay said, "I can attest to the fact that the longer they remain unresolved, the more difficult they become to deal with. It's always best to tackle these matters in a timely manner to ensure the most efficient resolution. Delaying action can lead to mounting frustration for the client and may even result in legal action. A tough conversation today is going to be way tougher tomorrow."

As a people-focused business, we prioritize building strong relationships with our clients, consultants, contractors, and city building department personnel. This is essential for creating a positive working environment where everyone can work together to overcome challenges that may arise. Trust is an essential component of any successful relationship, and we strive to maintain it with all of our stakeholders. When an issue arises, we believe that working together to find a solution is the best approach. By fostering positive relationships and trust, we create a supportive work environment that encourages collaboration and problem-solving. Our commitment to excellence and building strong relationships sets us apart from our competitors, and we are proud to be known for our high-quality work and exceptional customer service.

In addition to our production methods, we also operate on a fixed-fee basis. This means that we budget a certain number of hours for a project and strive to beat that number to ensure profitability. We also use refined metrics to plan ahead and staff projects and the entire firm correctly. Our billing is based on the percentage completion of each project phase, which is reported monthly by the project leader.

In the words of the grand dean of execution, Larry Bossidy, leaders must "be in charge from the start of each cycle, to the reviews, and to the follow-up steps you take to make sure the things that are supposed to happen do, in fact, happen. This is how you acquire both the knowledge and the authority to run the business as an integrated, reality-based whole. It is how you ultimately assure that all three processes are linked."

I close with excerpts from a strategic plan from our Phoenix office. This is from a few years ago, and confidential information is redacted.

Please provide the revenue goal and expected results for 2015 for commercial and interiors. Also, mention any major accomplishments and lessons learned from the year.

Some of the major accomplishments from 2015 include:

- Exceeding the revenue goal in September
- Largest business development month was in January
  - Successfully filling Lead Interiors and Operations roles
  - Not needing to lend labor out of office during the summer

Some of the lessons learned from the year include:

- Revenue generation from large corporate clients
- Dependency on large project waves for office revenue and schedule, need smaller stability
- Slow delivery projects are problematic and less profitable, seek quick and low scope for stability
- Commercial group is running smoother.

2016 FINANCIAL OBJECTIVES

Summarize revenue goals for overall office and by studio including revenue, profit, and headcount. Colaborate with CFO and senior leadership on targets.

PHX = $4.50 Million		
REVENUE	PROFIT	HEADCOUNT
Commercial		
$2.75 Million	$700,000	7 / 2 Interns (5 FT / 1 PT / 2 Interns) Interiors
$1.75 Million	$400,000	5 FT / 2 Interns (3 FT / 1 Intern)
$4.5 Million	**$1,100,000**	**12 FT 4.5 Interns**

ECONOMIC MARKET OUTLOOK

In your own words, write a brief economic/market summary for your specific market(s), and how it will affect your growth strategies. Please cite your sources.

The health of the Metro Phoenix economy is traditionally dependent on new residential permits. Residential permits remain slow but are recovering, with 30% increase this year and the same projected for 2016. The multifamily and infill boom is still strong in Metro Phoenix. The commercial real estate market recovery is trending with lower vacancy rates for office, retail, and industrial categories. It is expected to maintain slow but steady growth to recover at a modest rate in 2016. Historically Phoenix has kneejerked and overbuilt the market at the first sign of life. That surge has not occurred but is taking place in Nevada.

Industrial absorption is trending downward from 11.2% to 10.3% by end of 2015. Fewer new projects delivering, there should be some downward pressure through the beginning of 2016. Available developer product is thinning and locals are gravitating toward BTS solutions. *As a result developers are moving forward to position land and entitlements to clear the way for project wins.* Industrial fundamentals are strong and should remain intact for the foreseeable future.

Phoenix still has a large vacancy rate for office, around 17.6%; however class A product with desirable amenities (transportation, 67/1000 parked, high ceilings, +35,000 SF) remains in limited supply, driving demand for transformation of B product and new construction. Office rents are rising due to vacancies tightening and more expensive space being delivered.

STRATEGIC GROWTH INITIATIVES

In order to achieve success in 2016, it is important to identify key strategic growth initiatives for your office. These initiatives should focus on market share, product and service diversification, corporate account growth, and landlord building account growth.

Our expertise in MOB, Office, Retail, Automotive, Datacenter, hospitality and Medical are underutilized. Manufacturing and technology offer the most potential. Key talent has departed from Phoenix interiors in the past, but we are actively gaining new talent. WM Phoenix Commercial is strong, Interiors is growing, and graphics has been incorporated successfully. Site Planning services are used consistently and Civil Engineering is a local expertise.

In Phoenix, there is a need for a more balanced market share locally. This presents a great opportunity to develop core markets and new relationships. Major developers have been less active locally, limiting our exposure to other developers. Despite being in a retail town, our consideration in the retail sector is limited. Although the restaurant sector has improved, we lack a reliable corporate client. The most obvious opportunity for growth lies in manufacturing and technology.

WM Phoenix could greatly benefit from securing steady corporate accounts from companies. Initiatives for restaurant and industrial rollout have not gained momentum.

Indicate key strategic growth initiatives for your office to be successful in 2016. Make sure to address market share, product and service diversification, corporate account growth, and landlord building account growth.

ACTION PLAN TO ACHIEVE GOALS

In order to improve collaboration and leadership in the PHX office, a team-oriented attitude will be built through establishing workflow, expectations, and support from both local and far leadership.

- Identify and target leaders in each market sector, including Industrial, Office, MOB, Healthcare, Retail, Hospitality, Automotive, and DataCenter.
- Pitch brokers with a quarterly marketing package and build relationships.
- Host events, leadership meetings, and socials to encourage interaction.
- Develop an interface to promote collaboration between the commercial team and the office.
- Identify key hires or acquisitions to capture additional market share.

- Monitor market trends, pursuits, and transactions.

- Approach landlord/building owners with the WM PHX landlord program.

- Add a distribution or fulfillment corporate client and develop relationships with other WM markets to locate in NV, AZ, and UT.

- Gain exposure to aerospace, manufacturing, and technology pursuits via existing project managing brokers.

PLEASE PROVIDE THE TOP 13 LEADERSHIP GOALS FOR EACH OF THE FOLLOWING LEADERS IN YOUR OFFICE

Goals:

1. Grow a balanced team for PHX 1.
2. Secure international market share by being market aware and maintaining contact.
3. Energize and involve the international team by promoting the use of "we" and "team."
4. Develop steady corporate clients and absorb the WM way.
5. Maintain quality control.

Goals:

1. "Be Better" by growing a balanced team for PHX 1.
2. "Operate Better" by securing international market share and maintaining market awareness.
3. "Energize" and involve the international team by training and being a cheerleader for their success.

Master Strategy Class: Achieve Daring Long-Range Goals

> "First, think. Second, believe. Third, dream. And finally, dare."
>
> —Walt Disney

Walt Disney possessed a rare quality of dreaming big and daring to accomplish seemingly impossible goals while inspiring his team to do the same.* This quality of his reminds me of Leonardo da Vinci.

"Follow these four steps and there's nothing you can't do," Disney said. "First comes the thinking. Get this wrong and you're sunk. Think the right thoughts and you'll come up with the right idea to pursue. Then, believe like you've never believed before. Fall short on your belief level and you'll never make it. Next, dream of how you want it to be, right down to the last detail. And last but not

---

* Disneyland was scorned by the amusement park industry universally. "All the proven moneymakers are conspicuously missing." "No roller coasters, no Ferris wheel, no shoot the chutes . . . no carny games like the baseball throw." "Without barkers along the midway to sell the sideshows, the marks won't pay to go in." "Custom rides will never work . . . besides, the public doesn't know the difference or care." "It will never work."

least, dare to present your idea to the world and make it all happen in reality so you can benefit from it."*

Although Ware Malcomb has not yet reached Disney's level of success, our leadership team's pursuit of long-term goals has led us to new heights.

We called the company to these achievements:

- Mission statement: Committed to be the best commercial real estate–focused architectural firm in the United States.
- Revenue goal: Double the size of the company in five years.
- Locations/markets: 9–10 offices.
- Future locations: New Jersey, Inland Empire, Dallas, Nevada, Atlanta, Mexico, Toronto.

In 2002, Ware Malcomb achieved a total revenue of $20 million, which was a significant milestone. However, I believed that our company had the potential to become a national leader, and the economy was favorable. To make this a reality, I knew that we had to set new goals and test ourselves. So we gathered our leadership team and proposed a challenge to double the size of our company within the next five years. It was an ambitious dream, but we needed our leaders to be on board to achieve it. With their support, we created a long-term plan called the 007 Plan and set a goal to reach $40 million in revenue by the end of 2007. We worked hard on establishing specific goals for each office and strategies to achieve them.

---

* Quote widely attributed to Disney, not verified through Disney archives. However, whether verbatim or not, Disney preached numerous versions of this framework.

This was the first time we had created a long-term plan, and it was a great experience. It gave us something big to aim for and motivated us all to achieve this goal. Through strategic planning, getting the staff to buy in, and execution, we were able to achieve our goal a year early, earning over $42 million in 2006. By the end of the 007 Plan, our revenue had grown to $50 million. This was a significant victory for the company, demonstrating the importance of establishing ambitious growth objectives, clear strategies, and executing on them.

> **This was the first time we had created a long-term plan, and it was a great experience. It gave us something big to aim for and motivated us all to achieve this goal. Through strategic planning, getting the staff to buy in, and execution, we were able to achieve our goal a year early, earning over $42 million in 2006.**

We saw the power of creating a vision that everyone involved can buy into and work toward building. While the big idea came from me initially, many additional ideas and new processes that went into it came from the team.

As you know from the previous chapter, our path to 007 began by establishing the discipline of writing an annual business plan and being accountable for its goals. Once we became proficient at annual planning, we began to focus on the bigger picture: What does this add up to in the long term? What are our five-year goals? The energy and excitement from the team were awesome, and by getting everyone invested in our shared vision, we knew we could succeed.

Through the implementation of the ambitious 007 Plan, we were able to reinforce and enhance our company culture. We dedicated time to discussing the steps necessary to achieve our vision, how we can support one another, and where we aspire to be. The entire company bonded around our mission. It was crucial to obtain support and commitment from all team members and have them actively participate in the formation and execution of our strategy.

> The entire company bonded around our mission. It was crucial to obtain support and commitment from all team members and have them actively participate in the formation and execution of our strategy.

In 2008, shortly after we achieved our peak performance, the Great Recession struck. We had to navigate through the recession, and eventually, in 2012, we had recovered enough to consider the next big goal. We decided to write a new long-term plan, called the 2020 plan, with the goal of doubling our previous peak performance. Our first priority was to reach our previous peak of $50 million, and then to continue expanding into new markets using the same successful strategies we had used before, plus several new enhancements. Our ultimate goal was to become a $100 million company by the year 2020, which we achieved two years early, in 2018. It was the process and impact of the first all-hands stretch mission that made it all possible.

Leveraging Client Relationships

For 007, one of the main strategies was leveraging client relationships (LCR) to expand our business geographically. This also elevated our business with large corporate clients. In 2002, we began to look at the map in terms of geographic diversification and service line diversification. We suggested new markets to our clients where they had demand for our work, to expand our reach.

We started to build corporate accounts and leveraged those accounts by assigning **Layered Space Seating Group (furniture collaboration).**

an account executive to each of them. We knew that by establishing offices in new cities, we would build our corporate accounts and become more relevant to the Fortune 500, where companies require services in multiple geographic locations.

For example, during the 007 operation, our Boeing business expanded to eight different markets, United Rentals to ten regions, Toyota to five regions, and so on.

As we grew, we continued to expand and refine our corporate accounts program. Currently, we have hundreds of corporate accounts across our platform, which generate a significant portion of our revenue. Our strategy remains in effect: *diversifying our service lines and products to stabilize and expand our platform in important markets across the Americas.* These are our blue oceans and the main drivers behind our success.

Regional Growth

In 2002, we had eight offices (Sacramento, Northern CA, Los Angeles, Irvine HQ, San Diego, Denver, Chicago, and New Jersey). We took a deep look at our established markets and determined new areas of the market we could break into to obtain new business and focused on future locations in New York, Inland Empire, Dallas, Nevada, Atlanta, Mexico, and Toronto. (We updated these locations as we either established offices or changed course and added or eliminated locations from our map.) We established "WM Structure," a summary of different Ware Malcomb office prototypes to assist in planning and growth objectives. Parameters for each type of office included leadership objectives, management priorities, revenue and head-count benchmarks, market and geographic diversification, and LCR strategies and organizational structure. Our regional offices drove to expand business across all our service groups, such as:

- Master planning
- Office
- Industrial
- Distribution
- Medical
- Retail—big box
- Retail—auto
- Interiors

The offices fell into four classifications:

- Satellite office, focusing on core business, with the goal to become 80% architecture and 20% interiors;

- Small office, focusing on new core areas of industrial, technology, Class A office, auto, and graphics, with 70% architecture and 30% interiors and a goal of $1 million to $2,999,999 in revenue;

- Medium office, focusing on new industrial build to suit projects, office projects, and full service interior design, with 60–65% architecture and 30–35% interiors and a goal of $3 million to $4,999,999 in revenue; and

- Large office, focusing on new industrial, MOB, auto dealerships, interiors, technology, BTS, retail, and graphics, with 65% architecture and 35% interiors and a goal of $5 million+ in revenue.

With these new structures in place, WM expanded to new locations in our target markets. By opening new branches in these areas, we were able to increase our service offerings and market share. Our regional leaders played a crucial role in securing new accounts with established clients and expanding business in the interiors sector. These efforts enabled us to establish ourselves as a leading service provider in our industry, putting significant distance between us and our competitors. Furthermore, our impressive track record with our existing clients resulted in many referrals, which helped us attract new clients and expand our business even further.

Ultimate Ware Malcomb

As a company, we created a cultural phenomenon by consistently achieving our annual goals and continuing objectives. We have challenged ourselves to reach even greater heights by asking and discussing, "Where do we want to be someday? How can we think, believe, dream, and dare for longer, and set even more audacious goals?"

These discussions sparked a flash of light, and in 2007 I conceived Ultimate Ware Malcomb. It was a way to frame our progress as a step toward the ultimate potential of our company. If we are ultimately successful, this is what our company would look like, and this is who we are. It's a step-by-step approach supported by one- and five-year plans, and it requires discipline to figure out how to get everyone engaged and pushing in the same direction to achieve the common goal. The biggest piece of this puzzle is having the right mindset.

Ultimate Ware Malcomb is the embodiment of our greatest dreams, including a map, an organizational chart, expected revenue, and aspirational goals for our company. This exhibit outlines our ultimate vision and where we intend to go. It is not just a simple desire to grow, but a vision that extends beyond our yearly mind maps and strategic plans. It is an ongoing process that we are committed to achieving, in perpetuity.

Among the plan's highlights:

Mission

- Ware Malcomb is recognized as the best commercial real estate–focused architectural firm in North America by our clients, peers, and strategic partners.

- WM has penetrated all of its target major markets nationally and across the Americas. Each WM office has grown to a medium prototype with satellite offices reporting to it.

- We are in a position to effectively evaluate international opportunities and respond quickly to the markets that are ultimately advantageous to WM and our clients.

Innovation

- We have developed a continuous improvement program, WM 4.0, where employees can provide new ideas for company improvement and innovation.

- We look for new complementary lines of business that will create added value for our clients, and further separate us from our competition.

- We are recognized as the leading design firm for commercial real estate. We challenge ourselves to achieve the highest level of design on every project, while recognizing the client's financial parameters.

- We implement and leverage innovative business concepts, metaphors, and influences that enhance our company and our values, such as Blue Ocean, Leonardo da Vinci, Good to Great, and Freakonomics.

Culture

- We have a collaborative, team-oriented, people-focused culture.

- We attract team members who continually want to learn and grow.

- We are passionate about design, community, philanthropy, and wellness.

- Collaborative Idea Team Development: we keep the spirit alive at Ware Malcomb by encouraging creative leadership throughout the company, and we provide forums for expression and idea implementation.

- We pride ourselves on our strategic and cultural differences from our competition.

Enhancement

- We constantly innovate our business development strategies and marketing techniques, such as developing and leveraging broker education programs.
- Our compensation, ownership, and benefit structure are the best in the business, and enhance our employee recruitment and enthusiasm for WM, while still allowing management to be flexible as the company's needs require.

Of course, this vision could not become a reality unless we engaged the team to embrace it. We enlisted our leaders and asked them for their thoughts and ideas about how we build the Ultimate Ware Malcomb. How do we get there? How do we help each other? Where do we go? Many of the strategies came directly from the leadership team. We had them focus on and help write the business plan for the year. We trained them to have the discipline of expecting to achieve these goals every year, through tracking goals and being accountable to those goals. Once we realized we were very good at one-year plans, we enlisted the staff to help us figure out the five-year goal and, eventually, the ultimate goal.

We soon started reaching our goals on an annual basis and eventually crushing long-term goals. This type of strategizing is now a cultural phenomenon for us. The entire company now shares the Ultimate Ware Malcomb vision, focusing not only on short- and long-term goals but also on what it takes to achieve ultimate success. We have developed a step-by-step plan that encourages the team to get behind the idea and work together toward this common goal. It requires discipline and dedication from everyone to ensure we push in the same direction and accomplish what we set out to do.

Operational Imperatives

To be sure, executing a five-year strategic plan is a complex and multifaceted task that involves aligning the organization's resources, people, and processes toward achieving long-term goals. If you have digested and adopted the ideas in chapter 6, you're well on your way.

You need vision and drive from the CEO and senior leaders, of course.

You need to have focus and coherence around these behaviors while tailoring to the company, its business, and your workforce:

- It is essential to clearly document and communicate the strategic plan to all stakeholders, including employees, investors, and partners. The vision, mission, and key objectives of the plan should be articulated in an easily understandable and inspiring manner (Ultimate Ware Malcomb).
- Ensure key leaders and managers understand strategic goals and align individual/team objectives with broader objectives.
- Strategically allocate critical resources such as financial, talent, and technology to support the plan. Ensure that the budget aligns with strategic priorities.

- Break down long-term goals into short-term plans with specific action plans, clear timelines, responsibilities, and milestones.

- Of no surprise, invest in leadership development programs to ensure that the organization has the necessary talent to execute the strategic plan. Identify and develop Number Twos and rising leaders who can play key roles in driving the plan forward.

- Establish a regular schedule to review progress against the plan and remain open to adjusting it based on internal and external factors.

- Maintain open and transparent communication channels throughout the organization. Regularly update employees on the progress of the plan, address concerns, celebrate achievements, and provide clarity on any adjustments made to the plan.

- Develop strategies to mitigate potential risks and address unforeseen challenges.

- Engage with external stakeholders, such as customers, suppliers, and regulatory bodies, as their actions and reactions can impact the plan.

- Celebrate accomplishments and times when goals are met and surpassed!

A last piece of advice from Walt Disney:

"Everyone needs deadlines. Even the beavers. They loaf around all summer, but when they are faced with the winter deadline, they work like fury. If we didn't have deadlines, we'd stagnate."

7

Teams, Not Rivals: Building a World-Class Executive Culture

This chapter offers methods for recruiting and developing your senior leadership team. Ware Malcomb successfully learned from earlier mistakes and went all in on our company's values. And you can as well. Developing a team of leaders requires five essential practices:

1. Identify the values and behaviors that form the cultural foundation of your company as they support your operations and profits. This layer consists of the living, evolving elements that have made your company or team successful in the long run and cannot be easily duplicated. The most effective teams understand how to become integral to the organization, always contributing to and rooted in the cultural layer. A company cannot thrive without a vibrant cultural foundation, and for Ware Malcomb, leadership development is crucial for maintaining it.

2. Assemble a diverse executive team from within your high performers. Your executives should each bring new ideas and perspectives to company policies. Including different perspectives and regions is vital. By fostering a creative dialogue where team members build on each other's ideas, you can solve problems and make better decisions as a group. These edges between disciplines and skills produce the greatest innovation

and change, just as in the natural world. Collaborative *and* frank discussions and problem-solving lead to innovative and high-performing solutions. Interaction and freedom are crucial for sparking creativity.

3. Select each person carefully based on their performance and their ability to work collaboratively. Your senior leadership team should be made up of people who share your company's values and are committed to its success. They should also be able to work effectively with others and be willing to put the needs of the company first.

4. Provide your senior leadership team with the resources and support they need to be successful. This includes providing them with training and development opportunities, as well as giving them the authority to make decisions. Create a culture of open communication and feedback so that your senior leadership team can feel comfortable coming to you with questions or concerns.

5. Hold your senior leadership team accountable for their performance. This means setting clear expectations, providing regular feedback, and taking action when necessary. By keeping your senior leadership team accountable, you can ensure that they are constantly working to improve the company.

Ware Malcomb has a world-class executive team. I have been referring to them in this way for at least 15 years, and for good reason. The key is to recognize the power of empowerment and how it trickles down from the top. You may encounter fierce competition and internal politics among executives in your own company. However, you can uproot these issues by developing leaders who are committed to staying connected, helping one another, and nurturing future leaders from within. Aligning incentives with this philosophy reinforces the concept.

> **Ware Malcomb has a world-class executive team. I have been referring to them in this way for at least 15 years, and for good reason. The key is to recognize the power of empowerment and how it trickles down from the top. You may encounter fierce competition and internal politics among executives in your own company. However, you can uproot these issues by developing leaders who are committed to staying connected, helping one another, and nurturing future leaders from within. Aligning incentives with this philosophy reinforces the concept.**

Not every promising hire works out for your team, *which is part of your learning and growth process as well as theirs.* Or, in some cases, folks don't buy into our philosophy. We have had many talented individuals join our team over time, but some may feel overwhelmed or not interested in growing with us to the same extent. As a result, some people who helped us reach our current level are no longer with us. And that's okay, both for the company and for them to move on and find a better path.

Recruit and nurture your leaders as if your company's future depends on it. After all, it does.

Base Layer

Ware Malcomb, at its heart, is a leadership academy. We became a great company through compassion and focus on company culture driven by support, care, connection, and promotion from within. *What is your company at its heart?* The exercises in this book and your exploration outside the book's frame will help you answer that question and set a course for developing world-class leaders. *Cultivate leaders who embody company values and set an example for others.*

Ware Malcomb, at its heart, is a leadership academy. We became a great company through a focus on company culture driven by support, care, connection, and promotion from within.

What that means for Ware Malcomb is that our executives' and shareholders' commitment to success is defined by their continuous hunger for personal and professional development. Through their example, team members learn that scaling and taking on new opportunities and responsibilities is vital for the company and individual growth.

Late in August 2023, our senior leaders gathered to celebrate Jay Todisco's 25th anniversary with WM, and it was a memorable night. I sat back and enjoyed the conversation flowing around the large oval table, reflecting on the 25 years that had passed. (Celebrating milestones may seem old school to some, but I recommend being generous in this way because human beings thrive when we feel included and remembered.)

Each senior leader at WM possesses unique qualities and skills that contribute to the team's growth. Their collaboration and reliance on each other for support and guidance are remarkable. The team deeply respects each other, and their collective effort makes them exceptional. Witnessing such teamwork, dedication, and unwavering commitment to excellence is genuinely inspiring.

Each of our executive team members embraces personal and professional growth by taking on new challenges—the behavior that lies at the heart of our firm. They are always willing to step up and do what is required. CEO Ken Wink is an excellent example of this. He was tasked with opening our Northern California office and managing projects, which required him to learn how to run an office, lead people, and grow our market. After many years, he became the CEO. Similarly, Jay was moved to Northern California and then Chicago to take over those markets, which required him to learn new cultures and build markets from scratch, before returning to become president. These were major Chessboard moves for the company.

Our CFO, Tobin Sloane, joined us when the firm was smaller and scaled our financial operations with ease. He built an effective team and is invaluable.

Ruth Brajevich, our former marketing director, became a principal with the firm and served as CMO. She formed a top-notch marketing team and spearheaded initiatives by assisting in developing our graphics and branding department. Ruth is now Vice President of Strategic Initiatives, where she excels in bringing people together for long-term planning and special projects.

These examples demonstrate how our team is willing to take on new challenges and grow personally and professionally.

Maureen Bissonnette joined the firm in the late 1990s as an assistant and is now a principal and shareholder in the firm. "My tenure at Ware Malcomb has been a combination of good fortune, timing, and perseverance," Maureen said in an interview.

> My journey has been anything but straightforward. I have experienced three major economic downturns. Despite challenges, I maintain confidence in our unwavering focus on key factors for business success: strategy, people, operations, finance, and marketing.

> Since joining as a marketing assistant, I have been promoted five times, leading to my current position as head of marketing and principal shareholder. Employees really have the chance to contribute to important business decisions. The company values the growth of its workers and has programs to help them advance.

> My boss and other senior leaders have been incredibly supportive throughout my career at Ware Malcomb. Their encouragement and guidance have played a significant role in my success. Additionally, the company values the importance of work/life balance and trusted me with flexibility when I had my first child. I am grateful for the coaching and mentoring opportunities provided by the company, which have helped me and my team thrive professionally.

Our vice president of operations, Radwan Madani, progressed from being a CAD technical draftsman to a job captain within our project groups, eventually managing projects. He later took over and effectively ran our Los Angeles office for many years before returning to Irvine to take on the operations role.

Matt Brady joined our firm as an intern and later returned as a project manager. He played a key role in reopening our San Diego office, which he ran successfully for many years. Over time, Matt became a principal in the firm, and now he is an executive vice president and leads numerous strategic initiatives across the company.

Jinger Tapia is our vice president of design and a recent addition to our board. She started her career with us right after school, working in our design department. After a brief hiatus, Jinger returned and quickly rose through the ranks, eventually becoming a shareholder and principal in the firm. Recently, she was promoted to vice president of design and now oversees all our design activities, including our digital transformation team. As a board member, Jinger brings valuable insights and expertise to our organization.

Make sure that your potential leaders are capable of driving business growth. For example, a few years ago we acquired a civil engineering group, adding group directors and principals Tom Jansen and Chris Strawn to our leadership team. The group's goal was to expand civil engineering across the platform, and they've done an amazing job. When they first arrived, civil engineering was a small department with a presence in only three offices. Now, we have a presence in 18 offices. Chris and Tom are leading the growth of this platform, and Tom recently took on a new opportunity to become the regional principal of our Northwest region. Notably, a civil engineer leads a region, demonstrating our commitment to promoting strong leadership talent from within, regardless of discipline. Both Tom and Chris have now been promoted to vice presidents in the firm and serve on the executive team.

Ted Heisler has had an incredible impact on our interior design group at all levels. Initially, he joined as the director of our Irvine office, concentrating on interiors. However, he has since become a shareholder and principal after demonstrating his value. Promoted to vice president of interior architecture and design, Ted has taken charge of our Interior Advisory Group. Currently, he also manages corporate accounts and is working toward expanding them throughout the platform. Ted is a highly skilled, innovative, and dedicated individual who has gained expertise from multiple roles with the firm.

Over time, we've added several regional vice presidents from around the country to serve on our executive team. Homework assignment: You need an array of leadership traits, talents, and skills to make up your leadership team. Which employees are the role models in your firm? What behaviors do they exemplify?

Innovation at the Layer's Edge

I mentioned in the book that I use observations of natural systems to inform the layered leadership concept. The variegated layers of the forest, grasslands, and oceans generate vitality and regeneration. In an article published by the Loudon Wildlife Conservancy, Leslie McCasker writes:

> How the vegetation grows may be more important than the actual type of plant. Each type of vegetation represents a vertical forest layer: upper canopy, lower canopy, under-story, trunk, shrub, herb and below ground. Each layer provides places for nesting, hiding and feeding that differs from the layer above or below it. Different layers of the forest canopy have different temperatures, humidity levels, insect populations, and food sources. There are also different horizontal layers that entice animals to live in a particular habitat. For example, a river contains riffles, deep pools, and slow stretches that all have different combinations of food,

space and cover, and cater to different species. The more layers there are in a habitat, the more opportunities there are for a species. Putting it in simple terms—a more dense and tangled forest has a greater role in the ecosystem than does a simple, manicured lawn.[25]

Human beings also thrive when thinking and working in variegated layers. There is a bounty of insight to glean from this correlation. Variegated leadership teams create productive "edges" among themselves and their direct reports. Fresh ideas and mutual support promote performance, and performance is our goal. Our approach is to create opportunities for those that show ambition, perform, step up, and get our culture, without limiting who they are or where they come from. By fostering an all-of-the-above outlook on leadership development, you can achieve multivariate diversity.

> **Our approach is to create opportunities for those that show ambition, perform, step up, and get our culture, without limiting who they are or where they come from. By fostering an all-of-the-above outlook on leadership development, you can achieve multivariate diversity.**

Columbia professor and social scientist Dr. Heidi Grant, Dr. David Rock, and the NeuroLeadership Institute have published significant research on the value *of all types of diversity* to business performance, including an influential article published by the *Harvard Business Review* that found diversity leads to better team decisions.[26] The authors cited a study where diverse mock juries made fewer factual errors and corrected errors more often during deliberation. Financially literate people in diverse teams were 58% more likely to price stocks correctly in simulated markets.

Homogenous groups were more prone to pricing errors. Including individuals with different backgrounds and experiences in a team can lead to a change in the way information is processed to make better decisions, the authors found: "Though you may feel more at ease working with people who share your background, don't be fooled by your comfort. Hiring individuals who do not look, talk, or think like you can allow you to dodge the costly pitfalls of conformity, which discourages innovative thinking."

The top team in a company consists of the senior leaders, while the department level comprises the top managers. A wide array of skills, perspectives, talents, and learning styles among these teams leads to innovation and effective management.

I find that with different skill sets and perspectives, executives bring unique ideas and approaches to discussions about the direction and policies of your company. Design-oriented individuals, such as those skilled in 3D building information modeling, bring a different perspective from those focused on business development or financial management. It's also vital to consider representation from various regions and offices to gain important perspectives from different points of view.

> **I find that with different skill sets and perspectives, executives bring unique ideas and approaches to discussions about the direction and policies of your company. Design-oriented individuals, such as those skilled in 3D building information modeling, bring a different perspective from those focused on business development or financial management.**

Expect and encourage your leaders to be vocal about their opinions with each other and to their superiors as well; otherwise, the value of this strategy is muted.

Ilyes Nouizi serves as principal of resource services at Ware Malcomb and shared some illuminating thoughts with me in a talk about leadership philosophy. Soft spoken, insightful, with a gift for metaphor, Ilyes came to WM 20 years ago, and his growth in the firm taught him the benefits of "incorporating other people's experiences and building upon them."

As I reflect on my 20-year journey with WM, I am reminded of the invaluable mentorship I have received from various sources, both official and unofficial. It is clear to me that one cannot achieve growth and success by relying solely on their own experiences. Rather, it is far more advantageous to incorporate the experiences of others into one's own and build upon both.

In 2003, I began my career at WM as a production coordinator, which is considered an entry-level position in the industry. Prior to joining the company, I had recently immigrated from Algeria and had worked two jobs that did not provide me with much experience relevant to my role at WM.

Over the years, working in the resource group—currently the Production Studios—was not something many people chose to do and was not a popular career track. However, I recognized early on the importance of it for the company and decided to make it my blue ocean. Even though I didn't take official ownership of the group until 10 years later, I believe I made great use of that time, getting myself ready for that responsibility.

It wasn't tough. All I had to do was follow in the footsteps of the company leaders and everything they were preaching.

Ilyes recounted learning of "following before leading" as he was promoted over the first few years. He obtained his California architectural license and focused on producing high-quality drawings and meeting the highest technical standards of that craft. He sought knowledge from internal networking and company culture, as he tells it, particularly in understanding building codes and detailing. Ilyes became a production manager in 2007 and almost immediately was thrown into a teaching and development role as he helped new leaders navigate economic challenges during the 2008 recession. Ilyes had found a niche in operations, a distinct track for his career and his perspective on our work. That difference—his own blue ocean, as it were—made him a real player in how WM adapted to technical and operational changes:

> I decided to embrace and learn about the new emerging technology that was being hailed as the future, namely Revit/BIM.* As this technology became a hot topic in our field, our clients began to catch on, and it was important for us to not only remain relevant but also to become leaders in the industry when it came to BIM. Taking it upon myself to learn everything there was to know about this new technology, I went beyond that and customized my knowledge to fit within our company's needs and business model. This helped me immensely when discussing BIM with others who joined the company over the years and allowed me to make the best decisions for the company.

---

* Wikipedia: Autodesk Revit is a building information modelling software for architects, landscape architects, structural engineers, mechanical, electrical, and plumbing engineers, designers and contractors.

Once I was officially in charge of the group in 2013, there wasn't much time to rest or celebrate. The economy and our company were entering an expansion period like we've never seen before. And with that comes growth and all the pains that come with it. I quickly recognized that if the company continued to grow, one Ilyes wouldn't be nearly enough to manage a growing group, so I went on to find strong junior team members who would eventually grow to become leaders themselves. But instead of aiming to find one Number Two, I decided to develop multiple Number Twos.

Ilyes then navigated restructuring his division as Ware Malcomb organized the offices regionally; he continued to hire and develop his diverse team.

One thing I learned over the years is everyone learns in their own way, their own pace and style. There was no way to go through this in a group learning fashion. My mentoring had to be tailored to each candidate based on their needs and at the right time. I knew I had found the right individuals, so I decided that I had to take advantage of the situation and invest the time. I traveled a lot to expose people to WM culture and understand micro cultures in each region. Traveling with someone reveals a lot about them. Sharing my knowledge and experience helped my new leaders achieve their goals faster than I did. It was rewarding to see their progress and achievements.

Just as a puzzle is made of multiple pieces and the different shapes and colors that fit together perfectly, Ware Malcomb is made of team members with different backgrounds, experiences, and points of view, each playing a specific role to complement others, all making the complex puzzle that is Ware Malcomb.

> "Just as a puzzle is made of multiple pieces and the different shapes and colors that fit together perfectly, Ware Malcomb is made of team members with different backgrounds, experiences, and points of view, each playing a specific role to complement others, all making the complex puzzle that is Ware Malcomb."

On the Bus

I am a devotee of Jim Collins's *Good to Great*, where he observed "getting the right people on the bus" as a key finding from his research on what distinguishes great companies from good ones. The bus is a metaphor for the company, and "the right people" are those who share the company's goals and values. The inverse of this principle is that not everyone can stay on the bus.

When it comes to business, we often focus on our success stories, role models, and top performers. These examples are important for teaching and training. However, it's equally important to acknowledge and discuss behaviors that don't align with our company culture and explain why. Sharing and remembering these examples can help us create a more cohesive team.

Not everyone you hire will qualify for a leadership track, and that's okay. As people progress or have opportunities in the firm, their attributes show themselves. Many terrific professionals have focused skill sets that serve them well in their position. The Tinkertoy exercise we covered in chapter 2 is emblematic of the process for developing the broader skill sets needed for senior roles. Some wonderful professionals are happy in their niche. Many talented and prolific professionals aren't suited for leadership but committed to growing and developing in their niche.

Undoubtedly, we've brought people on the bus that had no business riding with us. Some individuals have struggled to work as team members, putting personal success and individual credit over the greater good of the team, department, or organization. This attitude undermines a core WM practice that involves serving client work spanning across different markets. When a client expresses interest in working with our office in another market, we encourage team members to introduce the client to the appropriate office and offer their assistance. However, we've had employees who attempt to hold on to projects and complete them themselves, even if it's not their area of specialization. This type of behavior is referred to as "revenue hoarding" and "ball hogging," which goes against our cultural values and the expectation of teamwork.

In an office setting, it's important for departments and service groups to collaborate and help each other out. For example, architecture and interiors can work together, while civil engineering can assist both. Building measurement provides a gateway to interiors, and branding opportunities involve all groups. However, if a group leader fails to act as a team player, they create a silo that goes against our cultural values. We've had promising hires who attempt to change our firm to fit their previous workplace, and this rarely works out. It took some trial and error to gather the fantastic team we have today, and those who didn't fit either left the firm or found positions elsewhere where they can thrive.

Sometimes, it takes a long time to find the right fit, and we have to test whether a person is the right leader for our firm. Sometimes, it's as simple as not being a great cultural fit or being used to different ways. It's experiential, and while there are formulas to follow, it's refreshing to be open to trial and error.

One of our offices encountered difficulty finding a suitable candidate to lead their interiors department. After going through 10 different leaders, we finally found an exceptional individual who we nurtured and developed over time. Despite being younger than most managers, she proved to be an outstanding leader, an excellent team player, and consistently performed at a high level. She has a long runway of opportunity in front of her. Lincoln, meet the new Grant.

We incorporate tools like CliftonStrengths to help us understand our employees better, but ultimately, our company culture is what sets us apart. When we promote from within, our employees are integrated into our culture and model it. However, when we hire senior-level employees externally, it's up to both the individual and the company to ensure they adapt to our culture and add value to our team. This also allows a senior leader to add a different point of view to the team. Our executive team and other leaders throughout the company are top notch, but they also had to learn and grow over time to become successful. We value teamwork and collaboration, and asking for help is never seen as a weakness. We aim to build on each other's ideas and make them even better. Our company culture is unique, and we want all employees, regardless of their level, to embrace it and contribute to our success.

Leader Support

Saying your company or team provides people the support they need to excel can be the corporate equivalent of "the check is in the mail," or "no new taxes." We all have limited resources and time, so finding practical solutions is important. One option is to hire temporary or consultant staff during busy periods, recruit more permanent employees, or extend deadlines when necessary.

Team members supporting each other is our secret weapon and should be yours. Our executive team works in a constant dialogue of support, including the CEO. Support is also evident in how colleagues help each other with strategies, financial issues, and life balance issues. We have support solutions available throughout the company, from production to marketing to legal and contracts. However, if any of these systems fall behind, people may not feel supported. Our IT system is also crucial as it needs to be available 24/7 to ensure that our employees can work without interruption.

> **Team members supporting each other is our secret weapon and should be yours. Our executive team works in a constant dialogue of support, including the CEO. Support is also evident in how colleagues help each other with strategies, financial issues, and life balance issues. We have support solutions available throughout the company, from production to marketing to legal and contracts.**

Although we don't have limitless resources, we have designed our system to scale based on revenue. We understand that deadlines can clash, and we plan for these scenarios by incorporating safety valves in our system. For instance, we outsource production outfits to provide extra capacity when necessary. It's worth repeating: expand your bench of outsourcing resources as your business scales.

Celebrate and appreciate your employees, please.

At WM, we hold social events such as Beer 30 Fridays, where the whole team can unwind and socialize, and team-building activities and art shows where creative team members can showcase their talents. Our biggest event is the company-wide holiday party, where employees and their significant others are flown in from all offices. We also celebrate achieving big goals, such as when we hit our 007 goal and gave out engraved iPods to all team members. We have a culture of philanthropy where each office supports a good cause in the community. Additionally, we offer regular training sessions called WMU on various topics related to our business and technical skills. We value our employees and strive to support them in their career goals. Our culture is focused on building a strong team camaraderie and appreciation for each other.

When extra capacity is needed on a major deadline, team members company-wide may jump in at the request of the office leader, the production studio, or the head of the design studio. We may ask employees to work overtime or reach out to other offices or outsourcing groups for assistance. While it's not ideal, sometimes we may also need to request an extension from the client. However, we always strive to meet deadlines and fulfill our obligations. When we fall short, we work hard to make up for it and maintain a positive relationship with the client. Our operations team is well equipped to handle these situations and works creatively and collaboratively to find solutions. It's important to have a strong team culture and leadership to ensure everyone is working together toward the same goal.

The Mission Beyond Darkness

The ultimate test for leaders is to support your team members and take on tough assignments alongside them. Sometimes, leaders must make sacrifices to support their teams at high-stakes times. At Ware Malcomb, board members and leaders take the first salary cuts during a recession. Many big-name brands paid all of their employees through the COVID-19 pandemic. While WM could not go to these lengths, in 2015, Dan Price, the CEO of credit card processing company Gravity Payments, made headlines by taking a personal pay cut and reducing his own salary significantly to raise the minimum salary of all his employees to $70,000 per year.

One memorable night in the history of World War II is still studied by military and leadership experts. During the momentous Battle of the Philippine Sea in the South Pacific in 1944, the US Navy decisively defeated the Japanese fleet on the first day. But the campaign was far from over, and late the following day, Admiral Marc Mitscher, with his other commanders, decided to launch an air attack on the vulnerable fleeing Japanese carriers. The implication was clear for every pilot in the US carrier group: the mission would require returning near or after dark with little fuel. Carriers ran without lights at night, and pilots interviewed later assumed this flight would be their last.

We also know that Admiral Mitscher, legendary as a leader of few words and decisive action, loved and cared for his pilots and their safe return and had survived an ocean crash landing as an aviator. As night fell, the news on comms spread throughout the carrier group of pilots making desperate ditches in the ocean, falling short of the carrier group.

Historian Robert Citino explains the difficult decision faced by pilots that evening. They had to decide when to ditch their aircraft—running on empty meant getting closer to home but having an uncontrolled drop, while ditching earlier gave them some power and control but left them farther out at sea. This was a tough situation either way.

In a dramatic turn of events, Admiral Marc Mitscher ordered the carrier fleet to illuminate in the dark Pacific night to guide the fliers to safety. This was a risky move as it went against standard naval operations, which emphasized nighttime-light discipline. But Mitscher was willing to take the risk to save his pilots. As dusk slid to dark, the entire battle group lit up to guide the pilots to their home carriers.

This event may seem like a miracle, but in reality, it was an example of higher commanders calculating and managing risk. Mitscher and his able chief of staff, Captain Arleigh Burke, knew the dangers involved but chose to prioritize the safety of their pilots. In the end, their decision to illuminate the fleet saved a large number of US naval aviators.

In the hour of utmost need, be a leader who lights up the carriers.

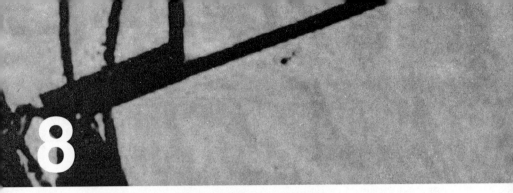

8

The Visible Light Spectrum

"Fall down seven times, stand up eight."
—Japanese Proverb

Welcome to the Visible Light Spectrum. It is a metaphor and process that can help you calibrate diversification in your business and maintain resilience during economic downturns. You can focus on your core strengths and diversify without mission creep by deploying the Visible Light Spectrum. This will help you stay on track and improve your business performance.

I've found the Visible Light Spectrum to be one of the most powerful tools I've shared at Ware Malcomb. Visible light waves are the only electromagnetic waves we can see, appearing to us as the colors of the rainbow. When all the waves appear together, they produce white light. The rainbow colors represent the core business where a company excels, as well as strategic, closely aligned diversifications. For Ware Malcomb, our Visible Light Spectrum encompasses the services we offer: architecture, interior architecture, civil engineering, branding, and building measurement services, all as services for commercial real estate. Just as importantly, it represents the commercial real estate product markets we design in: industrial, office, advanced manufacturing, retail, healthcare, science, and technology. It's a metaphor from high school physics class that asks: Can you visualize a business opportunity or new product market on your company's spectrum? Or is it invisible, too far outside the Visible Light?

On the Visible Light Spectrum graph, custom residential and government RFP work are at opposite ends (I can't see them). Commercial real estate is at the center of the WM Visible Light Spectrum, with our closely related diversifications toward the outer limits of Visible Light.

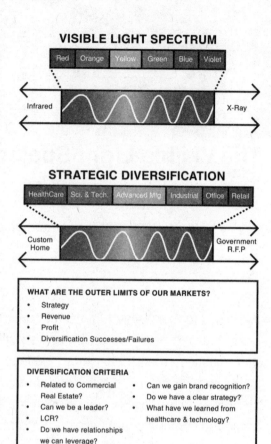

Ware Malcomb Visible Light Spectrum.

As a commercial real estate design firm, Ware Malcomb understands the ups and downs of the economy and the impact it can have on the industry. To prepare for potential recessions, the firm strategically diversifies its services and competes in closely aligned sectors that provide a buffer against economic downturns. This approach led to purposeful growth and national leadership.

> **For Ware Malcomb, our Visible Light Spectrum encompasses the services we offer: architecture, interior architecture, civil engineering, branding, and building measurement services, all as services for commercial real estate . . . It's a metaphor from high school physics class that asks: Can you visualize a business opportunity or new product market on your company's Spectrum? Or is it invisible, too far outside the Visible Light?**

This chapter explains how to identify a business's strengths—what you're great at—and communicate the necessary culture for success. Peter Drucker once said leaders should manage things but lead people. Sharing and creating a strategy to leverage your business's core strengths is crucial for effective leadership and the enduring prosperity of a business.

Leaders need to be bold explorers of new business opportunities that will diversify a client base and ensure income streams during hard times. The Visible Light Spectrum process delivers filters to help curious leaders make decisions, such as:

- How can your business diversify to sustain itself through all phases of economic cycles?
- Can you be a leader in this market niche?
- Is this possible diversification closely aligned with your core business?
- Is this possible diversification closely aligned with your core culture?

- How do you assess whether a new business line you are considering is a good fit for your business or business group?
- What acquisitions fit your core strengths?
- How can the Visible Light Spectrum enrich leadership?

Diversify for Recession Resilience

Most businesses are vulnerable to exogenous economic and regulatory events and must prepare for them. Recently we've seen government oversight and market oversaturation have cooled sizzling trends such as cryptocurrencies. The effects of COVID-19 hit the office market hard, especially with the advent of work from home that we were forced into in 2020 and the resultant agile work policies still in place in 2024. Another example was COVID's impact on the hospitality sector in 2020 and into 2022.* Hotel occupancy was severely impacted and did not recover until 2022. Restaurants diversified by adding curbside pickup and partnering with food delivery services, which became integral parts of their businesses.

Ware Malcomb's historical core strength lies in our expertise in designing speculative office and industrial buildings for commercial real estate developers. However, as experts in this field, we were also highly vulnerable to economic shocks. When the commercial real estate market suffers, the economy tends to follow, and developers put the brakes on projects. This was especially true in the early '90s.

---

* The *New York Times* published a fascinating and detailed essay by Anthony Strong on how restaurants can respond to price and supply issues here, including clever diversification: https://www.nytimes.com/2023/10/20/opinion/restaurantindustryshutdowninflation.html.

Jim and I recognized the need for diversification in our business strategy to make our company more resilient. We knew that by doing so, we could begin to mitigate the risk of going up and down with the economy and to establish a more stable business model.

During the mid-1980s, while I was in charge of the San Fernando Valley office, I was given the responsibility of creating interior office spaces for tenants of our client The Voit Companies. Voit was one of our most significant clients. During the previous decade or so, they had commissioned our firm to design approximately 50 buildings, including five high-rise office towers known as Warner Center Plaza and Warner Center Business Park.

At the time, we had never done any significant interior design work, but given the opportunity, we had to learn quickly and efficiently to deliver for our client.

As part of the project, Voit needed help filling up the towers with tenants, and they reached out to us for assistance with interior design and space planning. So we had to build an interiors practice from scratch, which was a challenge, but we were successful.

Interior architecture is a specific service in our industry, usually provided by interior designers specializing in designing fit-outs for office tenants. While many architectural firms offer interior design services, some firms only do interiors. We, on the other hand, were a diversified firm that offered both architecture and interior design services. Still, we were not known for interiors before the opportunity at the Warner Center project.

Eventually, we decided to make interior design a serious part of our business, given its potential and the fact that we had learned to be good at it. We wanted to grow and saw this diversification as a way to do that. So we invested in building that part of our company, and it paid off.

Looking back, I can say that the opportunity to work on the Warner Center Plaza project was critical to our success in interior design and diversification. It was drinking from a fire hose, and we had to learn quickly, but it was worth it.

Jim and I decided to make interior design an effort across the company. It aligned with our core business: commercial real estate-related design services, suitable for developer clients. It added recession resilience as the market timing between shell buildings and tenant improvements tends to be on complementary cycles. In this way, we could continue creating interior spaces for the buildings we had already designed, allowing us to work on the same projects for longer periods.

We then explored other potential areas to diversify into. Diversification is time consuming and involves trial and error, failures, and, hopefully, eventual success. So any new area we ventured into had to be related to business sectors we already excelled in, and we should see a path to becoming a market leader. I compared these diversifications to colors on the Visible Light Spectrum.

The metaphor of exploring unknown territories was powerful for our company. It enabled us to venture into new areas and discover our strengths (and weaknesses, more importantly!). In the past, we sometimes took on projects that didn't align with our values or expertise, such as working for the government or designing custom homes (I can't see them). We realized we needed to focus on what we were good at and find areas where we could excel and lead the industry. We identified our core strengths, such as commercial real estate and interior design, and explored what other areas we could add to our expertise. We didn't want to just dabble in different market sectors; we wanted to be a leader in every aspect of our work. We started adding advanced manufacturing, where we designed factories and assembly plants within industrial buildings. Then we added science and technology laboratory buildings to our portfolio. We took it one step at a time, building on our strengths and expanding our expertise.

The metaphor of exploring unknown territories was powerful for our company. It enabled us to venture into new areas and discover our strengths (and weaknesses, more importantly!). In the past, we sometimes took on projects that didn't align with our values or expertise, such as working for the government or designing custom homes (I can't see them). We realized we needed to focus on what we were good at and find areas where we could excel and lead the industry.

When we decided to venture into healthcare, we were fortunate to have secured a big project in the late '80s. We served as the architect of record for a large medical office building. As we progressed with the project, we discovered that the design principles we had already employed could be applied to healthcare buildings with some modifications. This realization helped us navigate the downturn and diversify our portfolio to include medical office buildings and clinics rather than hospitals, which are more institutional in nature and not as closely aligned to the commercial real estate industry.

Distill and apply these insights to increase your resilience:

Ensure growth opportunities offset economically sensitive cycles or customers. As with many of its peers, the huge ski destination Big Sky Resort in Montana developed and marketed a thriving summer conference business for professional associations and business groups and opened their lifts and slopes to dirt bike trails for competition and training as well as sightseeing. In 2008, during the devastating recession, Home Depot developed a diversification strategy to deal with the situation. They changed their slogan to "More Saving, More Doing" and focused on connecting with customers through lower prices and the do-it-yourself philosophy. The company also expanded its marketing to Hispanic communities and took several other steps to increase sales, such as:

- Implementing "Power Hours" between 10 AM and 2 PM Monday through Friday, when sales associates are available at the end of each aisle to help customers shop during their lunch hour.

- Offering a selection of 3,000 environmentally friendly products as part of their "Eco Options."

- Holding "Ladies Night Out" classes, which were localized in interest and geared toward women. For example, customers at the San Jose store who wanted to buy pricey tiles were given lessons on how to install them themselves.

- Providing free weekend clinics for kids, where they could learn how to build age-appropriate toolboxes, planters, derby cars, and other projects, with materials included.

- Conducting Do It Yourself workshops where homeowners are taught how to repair screens, paint, install plumbing, and perform other tasks that are usually done by professionals.[27]

In 2006, Walmart diversified and expanded its food offerings to include more organic and locally grown produce and meats to attract customers from higher-end retailers such as Whole Foods and Trader Joe's. It would later partner with former Whole Foods subsidiary Wild Oats as it expanded its organic offerings at substantially lower prices. This pivot was big news and had significant implications; the resilience of the move is what's key to know for our purposes. Walmart anticipated and addressed a loss of consumers due to a market segment migration toward the higher-end, organic market segment. It diversified into organic produce while undertaking changes in energy and sourcing to increase resilience economically and reputationally.

Tap existing in-house leadership and expertise. When an organization commits to the leadership development and training principles discussed in this book, your team can be a great place to find ideas for countercyclical diversification. I've said many times over the years that you learn everything in a recession. Just as we draw on our inner strength in challenging times, the same can be true of a well-managed business. The best ideas often emerge when we are undergoing extreme challenges. In the words of Helen Keller, "Character cannot be developed in ease and quiet. Only through experience of trial and suffering can the soul be strengthened, ambition inspired, and success achieved."[28] The writer David Powers observed, "Success is walking from failure to failure with no loss of enthusiasm."[29]

Ware Malcomb diversified into healthcare because, as noted, one of our architects had success in commercial healthcare developments and showed us how it fit on the Visible Light Spectrum. For years, Ware Malcomb resisted taking on multifamily apartment building projects, but through the leadership of several team members and their previous experiences, the team saw the possibilities for expansion.

We have had several clients who have invested in multifamily properties in the past and have been seeking our assistance for some time. With our confidence in our ability to specialize in this market, we have successfully increased our market share in the multifamily sector and are currently experiencing strong growth. During the COVID-19 pandemic, resilient companies innovated with new products, supply chains, and practices, resulting in lasting successes. As you'll read about in chapter 10, WM drove exceptional growth during that period.

From the mainstreaming of telehealth to manufacturing firms that fast-forwarded touchless production lines, the countless small businesses that pivoted to home delivery, and, of course, the installation of Zoom as a mainstay of human communication, we have tons of case studies to inspire and inform our own diversification planning. At WM, the resultant boom in ecommerce (into which we had diversified several years earlier) fueled massive growth during the pandemic. Ecommerce companies needed to expand their facilities quickly to respond to this increased demand. Our dominant position as the leader in design for industrial buildings, our previous experience with ecommerce buildings (which is very specific to each company), and our national and international reach provided us with a unique opportunity to meet the need.

Work Your Core

When you diversify, stay close to your core competencies and instill the strategy into ongoing operations and growth strategy.

It's essential for growing businesses that are considering acquisitions to carefully evaluate the expertise they're adding. I've seen companies make the mistake of adding businesses that have no relation to their existing operations, which can lead to difficulties in leadership style, management, and culture. For instance, my company diversified into civil engineering because it relates to all our projects. We didn't add mechanical or electrical engineering because we need to maintain the flexibility to hire experts for our different types of projects. Civil engineering is necessary for all types of buildings, whereas other engineering disciplines require specialized expertise. Therefore, we made a conscious decision to focus on civil engineering. I will explain in some detail as many businesses mistakenly hire too many top experts without having the clients to sustain the investment.

We specialize in designing various types of buildings, such as industrial buildings, high-rise office buildings, advanced manufacturing buildings, science and technology labs, retail facilities, and healthcare buildings. These different building types require specific criteria and requirements for their mechanical and electrical engineering. Therefore, we hire firms that have expertise in each of these areas. For example, we would hire a small engineering firm that specializes in industrial buildings to design the mechanical or electrical aspects of an industrial building. On the other hand, we would hire a different firm with an extra level of sophistication and focus to design the mechanical and electrical systems of a healthcare or science and technology building. If we had someone in-house who was a generalist, it would be difficult for them to be an expert in all of these areas. Also, if we hired someone who specialized in healthcare, they probably wouldn't know about industrial buildings as well, and they would be too expensive for the budget. Therefore, we prefer to have a stable of consultants based on their expertise that we can hire when needed. This approach gives us the flexibility to work on different types of buildings with other requirements. If we designed only one kind of building, such as schools, it would make sense to have engineering in-house. However, since we have a diverse portfolio, it's more practical to hire consultants. On the other hand, civil engineering is essential for all types of buildings, so we strategically brought civil engineering in-house. Plus, Tom and Chris have added immeasurably to our culture and esprit de corps.

There's another aspect to this. It is important to diversify in terms of the *services* you offer, not just the product type. After careful deliberation, we now provide branding and building measurement services as well. Ware Malcomb's civil engineering leaders hold a significant position in our company, and as an architect, I have always worked with civil engineers throughout my career. I believe it's crucial to not only obtain their business but also comprehend it. A real estate law firm may want to avoid getting into criminal law but might find success offering seminars in negotiating or construction trends. A marketing and PR agency I know well enjoyed success adding services such as social media services and event planning but does not pursue commercial ad placement.

To dominate and lead in any business, it shouldn't be too foreign to your company's baseline foundation. In our case, we focus on buildings related to commercial real estate. Therefore, whenever we consider expanding our company, we discuss how it relates to our current services, whether we can excel at it, and whether there is a demand for it in the market. A lot of design firms make the mistake of saying, "We do everything." We didn't do that, and neither should you.

Decision Prompts

Evaluate a potential business by establishing financial parameters, using a list of testing questions, and viewing it through the Visible Light Spectrum to evaluate fit. Use this list to assess diversification opportunities:

- Is the new project related to your core business?
- Can the firm be a leader in the market sector where the new opportunity is located?
- Does the firm have relationships within the market sector?
- What are the brand implications, from positive to negative?
- What is the strategy for meeting client expectations and gaining additional business?
- What are past insights from related client work? Share with the leadership team.
- Can you deliver services in this business competitively, efficiently, and profitably?

A Frame for Leadership Communication

It always comes back to leadership, and that is doubly true for the Visible Light Spectrum. The concept of the Visible Light Spectrum helped us layer our conversation around the direction we wanted to take the company. The Spectrum is portrayed in layers.

During a recession, people throughout the company may question why we are not doing the types of work our competitors are doing to stay busy. The Ware Malcomb Visible Light Spectrum provides an effective frame for communicating goals to leadership and through leadership to the rest of the company. I encourage you to explore the tool with your team and begin discussing how to fit the concept to your clientele and diversification decisions.

> During a recession, people throughout the company may question why we are not doing the types of work other companies are doing. The Ware Malcomb Visible Light Spectrum provides an effective frame for communicating goals to leadership and through leadership to the rest of the company. I encourage you to explore the tool with your team and begin discussing how to fit the concept to your clientele and diversification decisions.

Ware Malcomb continues to have discussions about diversification as we open new offices regularly. Our primary strategy with a new office is to start with industrial and interior design projects and gradually diversify into other product types as the office grows. Our strategic plans for each office include a focus on diversification. We have been using the Visible Light Spectrum as a tool for this planning process for the past 30 years.

Diversification by Acquisition

The Visible Light Spectrum is a helpful frame for thinking about external acquisitions (by service or geography—we've done both). We believe it is key to diversify and pursue growth opportunities that relate to (1) your corporate identity and (2) corporate expertise, because the culture of your company is tuned in to your core business. Bad acquisitions can become a virus that pollutes and weakens your culture, and even those that both parties embrace can pose significant issues of culture compatibility. Amazon took a risk with its acquisition of Whole Foods, and it came with significant culture clashes; however, the future looks bright after a transition period and a lot of hard work. The high-end, high-quality organic supermarket chain has invested substantially in the brand's values and commitment to quality and local sourcing, and customer loyalty appears even stronger.

According to a 2021 report by *Progressive Grocer*, Whole Foods has undergone a series of changes since being acquired by Amazon in 2017. However, the company remains committed to its mission of nourishing people and the planet. Rob Twyman, CEO at Whole Foods, stated that the company believes in its mission and considers it the right thing to do. Whole Foods has implemented several changes, including price cuts, ecommerce enhancements, and operational restructuring, but it has never strayed from its core mission.

> "Amazon still is who they are, and we're still who we are," [Twyman] says, "and yet we're learning from each other and growing from each other. With delivery, I think that's a great example of where we've leveraged the two businesses together. They've helped us understand through data the different aspects of our business, and we continue to bring philosophy around food in particular that I think is important as they continue to get into the food business."

> . . . For now, Twyman notes that Whole Foods' path to growth is not just paved with the highest quality standards in the food retail industry. The grocer, which last year had annual sales of more than $16 billion, also aims to win by focusing on hyper-local store design and merchandising, doubling down on its bottom-up leadership style, and expanding its 528-store footprint by at least 40 stores across 19 states and Washington, DC.

. . . To prove just how much Whole Foods is still Whole Foods, the company accelerated the evolution of its quality standards this year when it launched the Sourced for Good seal, an exclusive third-party certification program that supports responsible sourcing. The Sourced for Good seal is also designed to help shoppers easily identify products that meet the high sourcing standards required by the program.[30]

Bad acquisitions can be time consuming, expensive, and harmful for your brand. A few examples come to mind:

- Quaker Oats and Snapple (1994): Quaker Oats, a food and beverage company, purchased Snapple, a well-known beverage brand, for $1.7 billion. However, Quaker Oats had difficulty integrating Snapple into its existing operations. Differences in distribution channels and marketing strategies and a failure to comprehend Snapple's target market resulted in a decrease in Snapple's sales. In 1997, Quaker Oats sold Snapple for only $300 million.

- HP and Autonomy (2011): Hewlett-Packard (HP) bought UK-based software company Autonomy for $11.1 billion to expand its software business. However, in 2012, HP announced an $8.8 billion write-down, attributing $5 billion to accounting improprieties and misrepresentations at Autonomy. The acquisition was a significant controversy, and HP later claimed that it had been deceived about Autonomy's financial health.

- AOL and Time Warner (2000): The merger of AOL and Time Warner was meant to create a powerful media and technology conglomerate. However, cultural clashes (AOL maverick newcomer vs. Time Warner's "college of cardinals" elitism), overvaluation, regulatory issues, and the rapid evolution of technology all contributed to the merger's failure. The two companies ultimately separated, with Time Warner spinning off AOL.

- Sprint and Nextel (2005): The merger of Sprint and Nextel, two major telecommunications companies, was intended to create a stronger competitor in the wireless market. However, integrating their different technologies (CDMA and iDEN) proved challenging, resulting in network difficulties and customer service concerns. The merged company struggled to keep customers, and Sprint eventually shut down the Nextel network in 2013.

Huge corporate brands like these can sometimes weather the aftermath, but smaller companies likely cannot. If, as a business owner or executive, you can add a different kind of business, it should be closely aligned. It's important to consider: Will the post-merger org still feel like one company?

Diversification is the key to unlocking long-term success for any company. By expanding your product offering and branching out into new markets, you can reduce your risk exposure and tap into new growth opportunities. To achieve this, leadership plays a crucial role in guiding the effort. Your leaders must understand the company's mission and values and work toward building a business that reflects this diversification.

Ware Malcomb weaves diversification into our leadership meetings where strategic plans are formulated. New offices tend to be mostly built on the core business, so then they need to add diversification. At this level, we're not talking about inventing a new diversification. It's more like adding healthcare, for example, to an office if it hasn't been offered before.

In the context of a new WM office, the company as a whole has already decided on its goals for diversification. For example, are we going to layer in multifamily or civil engineering? Each office will have its own diversification priorities (within the WM portfolio) based on its respective market. The Houston office may layer in healthcare, while the Chicago office may layer in multifamily. The objective is to provide a comprehensive range of products and services in every company office, within the Visible Light Spectrum. However, each office has a mandate to seize the opportunities available in their markets to achieve this goal. If we expand every office in every market we aim to be present in, and if each office develops all the necessary products and services for their respective markets, and commands a strong market share, the company will be future-proofed against economic shocks as well as have immense potential for growth.

According to an article by James Schrager, a professor of entrepreneurship and strategic management at the University of Chicago Booth School of Business, "The lesson here is clear. However big you are, however successful you are today, however thoroughly you dominate your sector, plan for a time when your current strategy no longer works. Change always happens, and this means that strategies must be renewed and revised. Corporate leaders need to ask themselves: What is the pipeline? What is driving growth? What are we going to run out of?"[31]

Use the Visible Light Spectrum to see some answers, and a fleet of ships to respond.

Making Innovation Work: How to Embed Creativity Layer by Layer

You know about my admiration for Vince Lombardi, the subject of numerous biographies and studies in leadership, for whom the Super Bowl trophy is named. In what many call the Lombardi credo, he said:

> Leaders are made, they are not born, and they are made just like anything else has ever been made in this country, by hard effort. And that's the price that we all have to pay to achieve that goal, or any goal.

> And despite what we say about being born equal, none of us really are born equal but rather unequal. And yet the talented are no more responsible for their birthright than the underprivileged. And the measure of each should be what each does in a specific situation.

> It is becoming increasingly difficult to be tolerant of a society who has sympathy only for the misfits, only for the maladjusted, only for the criminal, only for the loser. Have sympathy for them, help them, but I think it's also a time for all of us to stand up for and to cheer for the doer, the achiever, one who recognizes a

problem and does something about it, one who looks at something extra to do for his country, the winner, the leader.*

According to Lombardi, leaders are not born; they are made through hard work and dedication. This same principle applies to creating an innovative company culture. Culture is developed, not innate, and requires effort from everyone involved.

> **According to Lombardi, leaders are not born; they are made through hard work and dedication. This same principle applies to creating an innovative company culture. Culture is developed, not innate, and requires effort from everyone involved.**

One Team, One Culture

In our system, leadership infuses layers of innovation into each department and function of the organization. The attitude of innovation permeates our entire culture. Why and how does that work?

Innovation is finding new approaches to existing problems and emerging opportunities. It is so *critically* a form of problem-solving. It is about developing creative ways to set an example for people to bring forth their best ideas and meld them into operational change and decision-making.

Innovation is an integral part of an organization's strategic planning and goals, more so than a designated R&D unit. When employees

---

* You can read a variation of the full Lombardi Credo here: https://dayton agonisclub.com/wp-content/uploads/2019/09/Gentlemen.pdf.

work together as One Team and bring their creative ideas to the decision-making process, it helps to build a culture of unity and collaboration. By understanding the bigger picture, employees can work toward a common goal, creating something greater than themselves.

Also, recognizing and bringing ideas to fruition energizes human beings and inspires them to continue contributing.

Significant brain science in the field of leadership points to the wisdom of nurturing innovation in every organizational layer. Creative energy is released by self-solving problems and being recognized for contributions. Everyone has their own unique creative processes that should be recognized, appreciated, and encouraged.

> **Significant brain science in the field of leadership points to the wisdom of nurturing innovation in every organizational layer. Creative energy is released by self-solving problems and being recognized for contributions. Everyone has their own unique creative processes that should be recognized, appreciated, and encouraged.**

Emotions are present in any human action. Emotions play a significant role in motivating individuals, and the brain responds much quicker to emotional stimuli. This can greatly impact a person's willingness to learn and their overall motivation. Feeling a sense of belonging and making a difference is among the most powerful drivers of engagement.

Additionally, humans are naturally inclined to cooperate with others to find solutions to complex problems. This innate desire to work together toward a common goal should be recognized and encouraged.

This is regenerative innovation, which fosters creativity and transforms the entire understanding of culture and leadership.

The Artist as CEO

We associate innovation with creativity and invention. Over the years, I've been asked many times about my career as an artist and my career as a CEO.

I've said many times that being an artist makes me a better CEO and leader, and being a CEO has made me a better artist.

As an artist, you have the freedom to create without constraints. However, in fields such as business and architecture, there are practical measures to consider and compromises to make. For example, when designing a building, it must be structurally sound, meet building codes, and provide for the functional and budget needs of the client. Despite these limitations, being creative and inspired as an artist can help one approach business and architecture in a different way. It can lead to more innovative thought processes and generate new ideas that can be applied to running and building a successful company.

Rather than choosing between art and commerce, it is exciting to synthesize the two. And any businessperson can adapt this lesson to their own careers. For example, at Ware Malcomb, we have built-in marketing and public relations teams that help me promote and market my art career. This is a resource that many pure artists don't have access to. When I find inspiration in the studio, my art often inspires ideas for business or another project (such as this book).

When it comes to finding inspiration for my art, it often happens when I am not actively thinking about it. Flashes of light can come to me when I'm relaxing, listening to music, hiking, on vacation, or even asleep. I make sure to sketch my inspiration as soon as possible to capture the idea. As you've learned, flashes of light have inspired me in art and business.

Once I have an idea for a new art series, I usually think about and refine the idea a bit before going into the studio. Then I tend to create several related pieces in quick succession. This approach to creating has also inspired creative leadership in my company.

Similarly, when the company needs to problem-solve or innovate, we bring the executive team together for an unstructured, preliminary discussion without a lot of agenda. An idea could come from anyone in the room that had an inspiration. The rest of the team will build on that idea and offer suggestions. Then we figure out the next step or steps and who will implement them and by when.

Creativity is served by keeping meetings short and to the point. Sitting in long meetings with long agendas wastes time.

Caddis (30" x 67" x 3"). Acrylic and metal.

Instead, I recommend exciting and fast-paced discussions that lead to action. As a result, your team feels emotionally excited and motivated to experiment and collaborate with colleagues across various levels of the company. Over the years, I have gained valuable insights from my colleagues and partners on how team creativity can lead to unexpected and productive outcomes.

Creativity is served by keeping meetings short and to the point. Sitting in long meetings with long agendas wastes time. Instead, I recommend exciting and fast-paced discussions that lead to action. As a result, your team feels emotionally excited and motivated to experiment and collaborate with colleagues across various levels of the company. Over the years, I have gained valuable insights from my colleagues and partners on how team creativity can lead to unexpected and productive outcomes.

The late Edward de Bono, one of the most influential authors and teachers on human thinking,* has been widely cited many times for saying that "creative thinking is not a talent, it is a skill that can be learned. It empowers people by adding strength to their natural abilities which improves teamwork, productivity and, where appropriate, profits."

All of us have creative impulses and activities. Later in this chapter, I will share some examples of how Ware Malcomb's people have delivered.

---

* De Bono's *Six Thinking Hats* introduced businesses to parallel thinking and became one of the most influential guides to "thinking better" in post–World War II history.

If You Are Not a Technology Company, You're Not a Company

Creativity is about building our business within the Visible Light Spectrum model. Innovation involves discovering novel approaches and solving problems. It also requires setting an example by developing creative ways of doing things in every facet of work. Creativity is an essential component of innovation, but it is not limited to that. It is a process of synthesis that brings everything together. Steve Jobs said, "Creativity is just connecting things. When you ask creative people how they did something, they feel a little guilty because they didn't really *do* it, they just *saw* something. It seemed obvious to them after a while. That's because they were able to connect experiences they've had and synthesize new things."[32] Well said.

> **Creativity is about building our business within the Visible Light Spectrum model. Innovation involves discovering novel approaches and solving problems. It also requires setting an example by developing creative ways of doing things in every facet of work.**

To achieve that synthesis, technology must be part of every process of change with which your firm is involved. In 2024 and beyond, if you are not a technology company, you're not a company. Leaders must emphasize that change and innovation require embedding capabilities like mobile apps, AI systems, and algorithmic tools across the business. Embedding these capabilities is an essential component to building an innovative culture. Activate your people in every layer with three deployment steps:

1. Encourage and reward participation; motivate everyone to come up with new ideas to improve your company. Frame the general themes, where the company needs ideas.

2. Solicit a variety of ideas. Some are easy. Some are harder. Some are great but harder to implement. Evaluate which ideas will make the most impact the fastest.

3. Then, as you implement, integrate the best technologies to reduce clunkiness and improve efficiency.

The Results

Ware Malcomb's encouragement of creative problem-solving and of nurturing a marketplace of ideas within the firm has resulted in a multitude of continuous improvements. The changes I describe below are the fruit of the innovation drive that began as WM 3.0 and continued at WM 4.0, 5.0, and WM Evolve.

As you will see, they embody layered leadership, emerging from various team layers of the firm, activated across functions and departments, generating excitement and motivation. Like a great rock blues band adding horns and strings, these changes add new instruments, new contributions, and new notes to the living culture of WM. Each section is a layer, and these selected innovations effect change and problem-solving in many, many ways. Some examples of great ideas we've implemented over the years (proprietary innovations redacted):

1. Workplace

- The office space was enhanced with the addition of Ware Malcomb–branded environmental graphics, which not only improved the visual appeal of the environment but also created a more cohesive and harmonious atmosphere. The graphics were strategically placed to complement the existing decor and design of the space, thereby enhancing the overall aesthetics and functionality of the area.

- Upgraded videoconferencing system and conference rooms to improve communication and collaboration among teams.

- Regularly evaluate workstation design and conduct office assessments to improve employee comfort and workspace efficiency. This includes assessing factors such as drawing table ergonomics, lighting, temperature, noise levels, and air quality, along with the placement of equipment and furniture.

2. Culture and People

- Culture Designed to Care Initiative: Company-wide initiative to create a caring and supportive culture that promotes employee well-being, satisfaction, and engagement.

- WM Active Program: Encourage employees to lead a healthy and active lifestyle through fitness challenges, wellness workshops, and other activities.

- #WMCrushin'It Team Member Recognition Program to recognize and celebrate team members' achievements and contributions.

3. Technology

- Creation of our digital transformation team.

- Use OpenAsset, a digital photo library, to manage and share project photos and videos more efficiently.

- The Hub Social Intranet Platform: Adopt a social intranet platform to provide a central hub for our team members to access information, resources, and tools.

- Adopt customer relationship management software to manage client relationships more effectively.

- Dynamo for Revit Capabilities: A visual programming tool to improve our Revit workflows and modeling capabilities.

How We Grow

- Ware Malcomb University regular training sessions provide team members with weekly training sessions to enhance their skills, knowledge, and expertise.

- Workplace strategy services to help clients optimize their office space for productivity, innovation, and collaboration.

- Offer building measurement services to help our clients accurately measure and document their buildings' dimensions and features.

- Offer clients an integrated services list for an at-a-glance comprehensive and seamless experience of WM services.

- Offer multistory distribution and cold ready industrial prototypes to our clients to provide them with innovative and sustainable solutions.

Project Management

- Developed a corporate accounts playbook to guide our team members on effective account management practices.

- Ware Malcomb PM Bootcamp: Provide project managers with a bootcamp program to enhance their project management skills and competencies.

- Regional operations structure improvements to ensure better coordination and communication between our regional offices.

- Introduce forecasting to predict and plan for future trends and changes in our industry and market.

Design

- Expand Enscape VR technology to provide our clients with immersive and interactive virtual reality experiences of WM designs.

- WM Envision tools to help our clients visualize and conceptualize their projects before they are built.

- Animation fly-throughs to showcase our designs and projects in a dynamic and engaging way.

- Developed Revit rendering standards to ensure that design visualization is accurate, consistent, and high quality.

- Utilize InfraWorks, a civil infrastructure design software, to enhance our civil engineering capabilities and services.

- Rhino 3D modeler to create complex and intricate 3D models for our clients' projects.

Brand

- Improved media and press strategy to increase our brand visibility, credibility, and reputation.

- Expanded thought leadership activities to share our insights, expertise, and innovations with our clients, partners, and peers.

- Developed a WM brand guide to ensure consistency and coherence in our brand messaging, visual identity, and tone of voice.

- WM Company Store: We offer branded merchandise and products through our WM Company Store to promote our brand and identity.

Vince Lombardi believed that weaknesses and areas of inexperience are opportunities for growth. It is up to everyone to accept this information and strive to improve. By making the decision to train and improve every day, even small steps can lead to giant leaps forward in personal and professional growth. This is the case with innovation, which, as Drucker says, does not come with the tempest but with the rustling of the breeze.

Lombardi Credo

Leaders are made, they are not born; and they are made just like anything else has ever been made in this country—by hard effort. And that's the price we all have to pay to achieve that goal, or any goal.

And despite of what we say about being born equal, none of us really are born equal, but rather unequal. And yet the talented are no more responsible for their birthright than the underprivileged. And the measure of each should be what each does in a specific situation.

It is becoming increasingly difficult to be tolerant of a society who has sympathy only for the misfits, only for the maladjusted, only for the criminal, only for the loser. Have sympathy for them, help them, but I think it's also time for all of us to stand up and to cheer for the doer, the achiever, one who recognizes a problem and does something about it, one who looks at something extra to do for his country, the winner, the leader!

Vince Lombardi

Part Three

Strategic Growth

10

Embracing Your Hedgehog: How to Master the Disciplines of Growth

This chapter provides guidance to help you transition from the challenges of building a company to achieving purposeful growth. The Hedgehog is a representation of the hard work and dedication required to build a successful business. On the other hand, the Condor represents the sudden acceleration that can propel your company forward to become a dominant competitor and stay aloft. Ware Malcomb has adapted Jim Collins's Hedgehog and Flywheel concept from *Good to Great* to suit the professional and creative services vertical industry. You'll learn how Ware Malcomb doubled its revenue during the pandemic and the surprising ingredients that enabled this growth.

The Hedgehog

Jim Collins's ideas of the Hedgehog and Flywheel concepts are crucial for the success of our business and many others. The Hedgehog analogy has multiple meanings that are essential for us to understand. We appreciate Collins's contributions, recognize their

GENERATED WITH BING AI IMAGE, POWERED BY DALL-E.

impact, and highly recommend reading his books. And we thank him for his inspiration!

As Collins discusses it,[33] the Hedgehog Concept is a simple yet powerful idea presented in the book *Good to Great*. It results from a deep understanding of the intersection of three circles: (1) what you are deeply passionate about, (2) what you can excel at, and (3) what can drive your economic or resource engine. To transform from good to great, one needs to consistently make good decisions with a Hedgehog Concept in mind, execute them well, and accumulate them over a long period.

Collins references the inspiration of Isaiah Berlin's essay "The Hedgehog and the Fox." Berlin divided people into two types: hedgehogs and foxes. The ancient Greek parable goes, "The fox knows many things, but the hedgehog knows one big thing." According to Collins, the leaders of the good-to-great companies he identified were, to some extent, hedgehogs. They used their hedgehog nature to develop a Hedgehog Concept for their organizations. In contrast, the leaders of comparison companies tended to be foxes, lacking the clarity that comes with a Hedgehog Concept and instead being scattered and inconsistent (à la Home Depot vs. HomeClub).

According to Collins, it is essential to note that a Hedgehog Concept is not about being the best, having the best strategy, or setting the best intentions or plans. It is about understanding what you can excel at and what you cannot. Every company wants to be the best at something, but few truly understand with clarity what they can excel at and what they cannot. A Hedgehog Concept gives the necessary insight and clarity to make these distinctions.

Collins writes,

> As you search for your concept, keep in mind that when the good-to-great companies finally grasped their Hedgehog Concept, it had none of the tiresome, irritating blasts of mindless bravado typical of the comparison companies. "Yep, we could be the best at that" was stated as the recognition of a fact, no more startling than observing that the sky is blue or the grass is green. When you get your Hedgehog Concept right, it has the quiet ping of truth, like a single, clear, perfectly struck note hanging in the air in the hushed silence of a full auditorium at the end of a quiet movement of a Mozart piano concerto. There is no need to say much of anything; the quiet truth speaks for itself.

From the early days, I saw the Hedgehog mentality as essential for WM and any company aspiring to excellence. Layered leadership is our Hedgehog. Doing the work of the Hedgehog makes breakaway growth possible. We adopted four axioms as the foundation of our Hedgehog principle:

- Axiom Number 1: New leaders should identify their most valuable market (LCR) niche and collaborate with colleagues to assess strengths and weaknesses in these relationships.

- Axiom Number 2: Focusing on client service is critical. Client service should always be our top priority. Losing a client implies failure.

- Axiom Number 3: Building the right team is vital. We should always have the best people in our group and continually identify and mentor our replacements. This is the only way to grow.

- Axiom Number 4: We are businesspeople. We must learn and practice the best business and management techniques and continually update our knowledge by reading business books, periodicals, and newspapers.

These axioms have been with us since the beginning of my tenure and Jim's tenure at the company. Throughout this book, I have discussed these important principles that have served as a foundation for our company's growth. These axioms have helped us build the company and continue to guide us in our operations. We must keep our heads down, work hard, and focus on what we do every day. This chapter will primarily focus on axioms 2 and 3, as 1 and 4 have been addressed in other parts of the book.

Some people make the mistake of thinking that the Flywheel (the growth) is the strategy. However, the Flywheel is a result of our efforts, not the strategy itself. We focus on our vision of where the company could go and let the Flywheel build on itself. *Within the practice of the axioms is revealed the Hedgehog mentality.*

Axiom: Focusing on Client Service Is Critical

It's crucial to prioritize client service in any business. When companies say they are "people first," it should apply to everyone, from employees to clients and industry partners. Although problems may arise, handling them effectively is crucial while ensuring that clients feel cared for. Honesty, transparency, and working in the client's interest are vital to maintaining trust.

Our baseline philosophy has always been to instill in our client-facing teams the importance of understanding our clients' goals and helping them achieve them. This applies to everyone from project managers and designers to the accounting team responsible for processing invoices and even our front desk receptionist.

Rather than focusing solely on our own goals or trying to sell an expensive service to our clients, we prioritize understanding their needs and helping them reach their desired outcomes. We believe this approach is the key to building lasting relationships with our clients and achieving success in our work.

One crucial aspect is being proactive instead of reactive by anticipating the client's needs and communicating with them clearly throughout the process. While our methods may not change dramatically, we know that certain pitfalls may arise on specific projects. We can build better relationships and trust by being up front with the client and not making them chase us for updates. If we encounter any issues meeting a deadline, our goal is to communicate with the client early and clearly explain the situation and what we are doing to resolve it. Emphasizing these client-centered approaches is critical to how we do business, and we reinforce these concepts through our mentoring and training programs.

Ware Malcomb offers a boot camp for project managers and job captains. It's a training program where we teach our project managers about our processes and expectations when managing projects. If you're new to the position or just got promoted, it helps you understand your role and responsibilities. We have this training a few times yearly, providing valuable learning opportunities.

In addition to WM Boot Camp, we also have WM Cultivate, which includes a class designed to train new leaders. For instance, if someone is a project manager in an office and is getting promoted into a leadership position via the studio manager or a new director, WM Cultivate can teach them how we want leadership to happen at our company. They will learn how to build and grow a team, handle clients, and ensure quality control.

Another program we have is Ware Malcomb University (WMU), a virtual weekly training available to all team members on a wide variety of topics, including technical skills, growth, and health.

To inform your ideas, other WM programs to promote personal and professional development include:

- WM Emerging Leaders (ELP): This annual cohort-based program identifies high-performing and high-potential team members and enhances their leadership skills through education, engagement, and personal and professional development. A rotating group of WM leaders engages learners through personal development assessments, group activities, and panel discussions. The 2023 ELP Cohort comprised 24 team members from 14 Ware Malcomb offices.

- WM Mentoring Program: As discussed earlier in our book, this company-wide mentorship program was developed in 2012 to provide team members with one-on-one coaching and guidance from experienced leaders throughout Ware Malcomb. Over 1,000 team members have participated in the program, resulting in an inclusive program that engages over 35% of the team members annually.

- WM CliftonStrengths: Ware Malcomb believes that discovering and developing unique talents makes team members more successful. To achieve this, each team member is provided with a copy of CliftonStrengths, and a specialized report is generated with their Top Five Strengths. Webinars are also hosted to further support team members leveraging their strengths to thrive.

Axiom: Building the Right Team Is Vital

Building the right team is equally important. Hiring the right people and committing to their growth and success is critical. We've demonstrated this allegiance in various ways throughout our company's history.

Some leaders at other companies are afraid to embrace the idea of empowerment and building up their people. However, nurturing the temperament to hire supersmart people and empower and guide them is essential. By doing so, you tap into more talent, energy, and aspirational drive to achieve the company's, unit's, or team's mission. Hiring intelligent people also fosters a nimble culture as the company grows.

You can't hire a grab bag of superstars to make you a Condor. It doesn't work in sports teams, and it won't work on your team. Building a world-class corps of leaders is about patience, time, and education. It's the Ware Malcomb way, and can be yours as well, driven by a sustained focus on leadership development day after day, week after week, month after month.

Remember the Chessboard? The concept empowers you to tailor your organizational chart and mission to achieve success by analyzing and providing opportunities for new leaders where they will be most effective. When we establish a new office, we ensure we have a skilled and experienced leader who believes in our program, culture, and mission and can inspire their team to do the same. Our office leaders must exude these qualities every day to their team members. It's helpful to consider leadership development concepts as layers that are synthesized into your culture and growth strategy.

Starting a new office or diversifying an existing one can provide numerous leadership opportunities. These chances can help fulfill the mission of creating as many growth opportunities as possible for employees. I was fortunate to receive an opportunity that helped me advance my career. So I am committed to providing those to others.

The Condor

The Flywheel's and the Condor's flights are not easy to achieve. Growth of this quality is earned by doing a great job, synthesizing layered leadership concepts, and implementing ideas like blue ocean and our axioms while keeping the entire philosophy in mind. It doesn't just happen because you want it to.

We've touched on LCR, leveraging client relationships, as a strategy that allows companies to transfer client relationships between different parts of their organization. Our LCR program with our development and Fortune 500 clients, especially, is an excellent example of how we work. When we open or build an office or have an office that isn't doing work with a particular client but we've done successful work for this client elsewhere or in several markets, it becomes easier for the client. *The key is to eliminate friction for the client.*

It is much easier for clients to work with us than to hire another firm in a new market. We already know the preferences of the clients, their contracts, invoicing procedures, particular specs, and details they use on their projects. This makes it easier for the clients to work with us in different markets, and our corporate account and LCR programs further simplify the process. We have a saying that "the phone just rings," and we get opportunities that come to us that we did not necessarily go after. This is because our name is out there, clients have seen our work, and they call on us to work with them. However, all of this is only possible with excellent customer service, the Hedgehog mindset, and the implementation of the philosophy in this book. When an opportunity arises, we can promote someone to lead our group or office and tap the strength of our platform.

Having the right combination of a good leader with the right skill sets and contacts in each market is crucial. When these leadership attributes are combined with the strength of our platform, it sets the Condor into flight, a rising sustainable growth rate lifting us above the competition. Our results are a direct outcome of our consistent hard work, and we must never forget it. We cannot assume that the Condor will continue to soar or that the Flywheel will continue to spin on its own, as it requires us to put in our best efforts daily. We must continue to work hard and strive for excellence, just as we always have, to ensure that the Condor gains altitude.

This is what Jim Collins meant in his book, and there is no doubt that the Condor will soar once we keep doing our best.

When success finally comes, it feels incredible, almost like a dream come true. However, it is essential to always remember the fundamentals that helped you achieve that success. You must keep working hard and never give up. You have to stay focused and committed, just like the Hedgehog.

Unfortunately, many successful people tend to lose their way because they start thinking they are invincible and that the world owes them everything. This attitude is dangerous and can lead to their downfall. It's important to stay humble and grounded and avoid letting your ego take control.

One such example is the case of Samuel Bankman-Fried, who thought he could raid his hedge fund for his own use and mask losses in the cryptocurrency exchange FTX without any consequences. Eventually, it failed spectacularly, and SBF was arrested, tried, and convicted. It's sad to see such things happen, but it's a reminder that you can't take anything for granted. You have to keep working hard every day and never stop learning. Success is earned, not given, and it requires constant effort to maintain it.

I have witnessed people within and outside our industry who believe that success is solely about their individual contributions. However, this could not be further from the truth. Success is a team effort that involves a combination of factors such as strategy, culture, the philosophy, the platform, and the talented individuals within the company. It is crucial to understand that if one person thinks it is all about them, it is destined for failure. It is essential to cultivate a culture of humility and remind ourselves that we are lucky to be a part of a phenomenal company supported by many incredible people.

Determining whether a company values empowerment without knowing the existing culture is challenging. Embracing the idea of empowerment is crucial to creating a healthy work culture. It requires humility to hire people who are smarter and better at certain things than oneself, possessing capabilities and talents that one lacks. It's important to empower and guide those individuals by providing necessary resources such as training, mentoring, coaching, and guidance. Empowering people involves allowing them to fail and learn from their mistakes, creating growth opportunities.

People respond differently based on their career and life circumstances, so it is not a straight line. However, empowering people and letting them go while guiding them without micromanaging is crucial. Trusting them and making them feel empowered is the key to unlocking their full potential, and they will undoubtedly accomplish incredible things.

One of the best pieces of advice I ever received on delegation was from one of my early jobs as a sixteen-year-old working in a deli and sandwich shop. I had a couple other kids I was supervising during the afternoon shift. Marty was the owner, a hardworking guy, and huge Cleveland Browns fan who enjoyed talking to the customers. He told me, "Delegate, don't abdicate." This lesson has stayed with me throughout my career. There is a fine line between being a micromanager and empowering people. It's important to provide guidance, regular check-ins, and accountability while allowing new team members to take on new responsibilities.

Some people believe that it's more efficient to do things themselves rather than teach others how to do them. However, this approach is not beneficial for anyone involved. It's not efficient for the manager to do tasks that their team members should be doing. Moreover, their team members won't be empowered to grow and advance in their careers.

Delegate, don't abdicate. This is an art and a learned skill.

As discussed earlier, we have specific metrics, growth goals, and strategic plans. However, sometimes business units or offices may not be able to achieve them, while at other times, they may exceed them. It all depends on their location and the nature of their work.

Regardless of the outcome, it presents an opportunity for learning and growth.

Regarding problem-solving, management consultants are sometimes brought in to apply a temporary solution without addressing the underlying issue. However, quick fixes and "Hail Marys" may not always be practical or intuitive. It is crucial to approach the problem with caution and aim to identify the root cause.

If a company needs to implement a cultural change to achieve its vision, it's essential to focus on the central idea that drives the change. However, this process requires long-term commitment and hard work. Success is built on top of success, and it's essential to integrate and synthesize new ideas that support the company's overall vision and philosophy. This is the approach you've explored in this book—a synthesis of ideas that come together to create a cohesive and sustainable plan for success.

Simply injecting one idea, such as a 360-degree feedback model, into a bad culture will not work. The concept must fit in with the organization's overall culture and fundamental philosophy. We have learned a lot from various business books and examples of successful companies, but we have always customized them to fit our needs. We have made them our own by adding our unique touch, just as we did with blue ocean and other concepts.

Understanding that what works for one company may not work for another is crucial. Every company has its own culture, vision, and way of doing things. However, if you have a strong culture and concept, it is possible to take some ideas from other organizations and modify them to fit your needs.

The Recession

President John F. Kennedy memorably said in his 1962 State of the Union address that the time to replace the roof is when the sun is shining.

That is the approach we took over the years before growth indeed took flight. For instance, the Great Recession was tough on everyone, including our company. We had to downsize and learn to focus on our most resilient business segments, such as industrial. We also worked hard to build our corporate accounts, a process that had been ongoing for a long time. This paid off as we secured more business from Fortune 500 companies and other large firms.

All this preparation helped us when the pandemic hit. Several of our biggest clients, who were involved in ecommerce, benefited greatly from the pandemic. Thanks to our prior efforts, we were already a top choice for these clients.

We had been working hard for years—grinding and digging away like a Hedgehog. We never could have predicted the success of our Flywheel. Ecommerce had been growing steadily and was set to continue, but the pandemic caused it to explode. With everyone stuck at home, online shopping became necessary. This unexpected boom affected some of our manufacturing clients who provide masks and other equipment that was so needed at the time and also companies with an ecommerce platform. We were fortunate to be already working with these companies and had the capacity to assist them as they grew. We were lucky, of course, but there was also a solid strategy behind our success that we would have continued to build on with or without the pandemic. It all comes down to our commitment to our plan, customer service, and core values.

When facing rapid growth, how can leaders anticipate challenges in their development? The challenge lies in performing and delivering results quickly. We rely on concepts like the Road Runner and Coyote to meet this challenge. The Coyote, which represents operations, becomes critical in ensuring that everything runs smoothly. During our rapid growth, we had to perform and deliver results, which required more internal communication and attention to detail. We made sure we had strong leadership and committed team leaders who were able to communicate effectively. We also hired some great people during this time, which was beneficial for everyone involved. Ultimately, communication, strong leadership, and committed team leaders helped us overcome the challenges of rapid growth.

During this time, we doubled the size of our business, so we had much to lose if our people did not commit to our values and system. To recap, when the Flywheel spins, and double-digit growth takes flight, the following are critical:

- A trained, veteran leadership team;
- Thoroughly tested customer service and customer experience practices;
- A training pipeline;
- Established communication protocols and practices: supervisor to supervisor, supervisor to direct report, unit to unit, leader to leader, team member to client, team member to vendor; and
- Strong operations leadership and communication channels to sales or business development.

It is important to remember that even well-meaning peers, consultants, or employees may try to persuade you to stray from focusing on your area of expertise and instead expand into profitable but unfamiliar markets or projects. Stay focused on your core strengths and Hedgehog your patch of greatness.

Exploration Sketchbook: Read *Good to Great*, and identify your Hedgehog, expressing your ideas in written and graphic form. What is your zone of greatness?

One Team, Many Markets: Layering
Strategies for Sustainable Expansion

Thank you for joining me on this journey toward purposeful growth.
In chapter 9, we explored regenerative and problem-solving innovation. In chapter 10, we learned about the power of the Hedgehog
Concept, which helps us focus on our core strengths. In this chapter, we will be exploring the expansion into new geographical markets and external acquisitions. While Ware Malcomb and many
profitable companies emphasize growth from within over acquisitions, the philosophy of purposeful growth means choosing growth
opportunities that meet financial goals and fit your culture. Establishing operations in new geographic markets bridges internal and
external strategies.

> **Establishing operations in new geographic markets bridges
> internal and external strategies.**

Many businesspeople I meet, and I'm sure many of you, have
undertaken, or are in search of, effective approaches for driving
geographical expansion that make sense for a company's skills
and resources. There are very few businesses that should com-
pletely disregard the potential of expansion, whether it is within the

local vicinity or in far-reaching locations. For us, this includes market sectors in design such as industrial and logistics (of course), corporate office buildings, interior design, retail, restaurants and hospitality, manufacturing, science and technology, and healthcare (medical office buildings, ambulatory care centers, surgical outpatient facilities).

Many of us want growth, already have clients in regions that are not our home market, and possess the passion and expertise to serve those clients effectively. Expansion is also a tempting new chapter to add to your brand story. But success comes down to answering the fundamental questions for understanding and executing any strategy: How, where, when, and why do we carry out the decisions? How do we manage our resources and avoid overspending?

Ware Malcomb, which started as a regional Southern California design firm, is now a successful powerhouse with over 1,000 employees across the Americas in 28 markets from Seattle to São Paolo. We have received recognition several times as a fastest-growing private company and a Hot Firm by Zweig Group. The firm is also ranked among the top 15 architecture/engineering firms in *Engineering News-Record*'s Top 500 Design Firms and the top 25 interior design firms in *Interior Design* magazine's Top 100 Giants. We have been honored several times in the Inc. 5000.

We've done this by never losing sight of the Visible Light Spectrum.

We've done this by understanding our strengths and prioritizing our company culture and values while expanding to new markets based on client demand and strategic feasibility.

We've done this by refining and updating our approach day to day, month to month, year to year. Among the topics I'll address here are:

- How leadership monitors and updates a map of target markets focusing on commercial real estate development and essential markets for corporate America.

- Why local offices are essential for effective client service and business development in a particular market.

- How to open a new office phase by phase, including finding a suitable location and ramping up staff.

- Why building relationships and trust takes time in new markets.

- How to assess acquisition targets based on work similarity, cultural fit, and willingness to engage.

- How our internal teams handle post-acquisition integration, with the CEO, president, CFO, and regional vice presidents all involved.

Client Demand and Market Potential

Client interest and service drove the first stage of Ware Malcomb's expansion efforts. We were often invited to join markets with thriving commercial real estate industries, where our clients were active and required our assistance. This was true when Bill and Bill opened the San Diego (which Jim ran) and Warner Center offices (which I ran), respectively. Jim and I then opened the Northern California and Denver offices and several others in response to the encouragement of our long-standing client Ted Antenucci, CEO, Catellus Development Corporation, and the support of many other important clients.

We used to choose our locations based on the requests of our clients or our knowledge of a particular market where a group of clients had a strong presence. Sometimes we would even ask our clients if establishing a presence in a particular location would be helpful. However, we soon became more proactive in our approach and identified priorities for our next locations as work came to us. If we had multiple projects in a particular market, as well as several existing and target clients, we would establish a presence there.

> **We developed a strategic map to identify markets with a strong commercial real estate industry . . . where our clients were active, and where there was a gap in the market.**

As Ware Malcomb expanded further, we began strategizing where to go next. We learned to integrate our offices into the company using the "One Team approach," which we continue to refine. We developed a strategic map to identify markets with a strong commercial real estate industry, as well as Fortune 500 footprints, where our clients were active, and where there was a gap in the market. Then we prioritized the cities we wished to expand to and decided which ones to pursue. Ware Malcomb leaders are still building on this map and identifying more growth opportunities for the company and our employees.

The expansion map is a shared commitment, a living document, that informs decisions about where the company invests its resources.

To solidify your planning for expansion, it's important to consider several significant factors. One of them is tapping into existing relationships with regional players in your industry. This can help you gain valuable insights and build strong partnerships.

Another factor to consider is compiling economic, industry, and socioeconomic trend data as part of your feasibility study. There are a number of platinum standard information sources that can help you with this, including the Bureau of Economic Analysis at the US Commerce Department, Data USA (one of the least appreciated but most powerful data sources available in assessing socioeconomic and demographic trends on city-by-city and county-by-county bases), St. Louis Federal Reserve (FRED) regional economic data, StatsAmerica (a joint project of the US EDA and the Kelley School of Business), the US Regional Data Project at the St. Louis Fed, the US Census Bureau, the Occupational Outlook Handbook at the US Bureau of Labor Statistics, and Employment Projections and related reports at the US Bureau of Labor Statistics. By leveraging these sources, you can better understand the economic and industry landscape and make more informed decisions.

WM has national relationships with commercial brokerage firms such as CBRE, JLL, and several others. When considering entering in a new market, we meet with representatives of these firms and others, gather referrals from those companies, and ask them about the market. We want to understand the long-term viability of the commercial real estate market in that area. We study this from multiple sources, and the team overseeing the new office provides leaders with a strategic feasibility report. They gather information from the commercial real estate brokerage industry, contractors, developers, and our corporate clients. We consider factors like competition, strengths and weaknesses of our competitors, the labor pool, and more. The report is then presented to the CEO and president, who make a decision based on business needs and who can be assigned to send into that market. This is how we decide whether to proceed.

> When considering being in a new market, we meet with people in that market, gather referrals from those companies, and ask them about the market. We want to understand the long-term viability of the commercial real estate market in that area.

If the leadership team decides to move forward, WM will start planning the next steps. This involves figuring out a timeline and assessing if there is any work in the new market. If so, we will speak to those clients to understand the market better and explore opportunities to expand our work. We will then identify the right leadership for this new venture, whether it be someone from within the company or through the hiring process. We will also search for the best location for our new office space, normally in an area where our clients and industry partners are located.

The Organic Growth Layer

The search for the best location considers factors such as accessibility, convenience, and cost. The location of the office could have a significant impact on success in the new market, so take the time to find the best possible location based on your industry and market.

An important aspect of establishing a new remote office is to pair WM culture with local knowledge and relationships. When we move a WM leader into a market to develop the office (Chessboard), we then hire local talent to assist with local knowledge and relationships. Conversely, when we hire a local leader to start up the office, we will move a WM team member to assist with WM cultural knowledge, policies, procedures, and resources. This approach has been successful in the past, and I know that it will continue to be effective for Ware Malcomb as we expand into new markets. It can work for you as well.

Local Knowledge

When it comes to providing services to clients, some companies prefer to have their employees work from a central office, sending them out to different locations as needed. For example, consultancies might send their staff to a particular client location for three days a week. Some design firms will travel to client worksites when the final architectural plans are being developed. However, in our experience, this approach is less effective than having offices in key locations.

Having leaders under the WM banner who understand the local building departments, real estate organizations, and associations is essential for providing excellent customer service, developing strong relationships with clients, and ensuring that projects meet local regulations. Simultaneously, accessing the resources of a larger organization is necessary to provide high-quality work and achieve a significant market share in a specific area.

> **Having leaders under the WM banner who understand the local building departments, real estate organizations, and associations is essential for providing excellent customer service, developing strong relationships with clients, and ensuring that projects meet local regulations.**

While we do work in markets where we don't have an office, we find that once we begin to build market share, having a local presence is the most effective way to serve our clients and achieve our long-term goals. That's why we have offices in key locations throughout North America.

When a new leader, whether internal or external, takes charge of the office, a specific day is marked on the calendar for their arrival. Ideally, the office space is ready to go.

The new manager's onboarding process will depend on whether they are an internal hire or someone we've recruited externally. In case of an internal hire, they will need to familiarize themselves with the local community and market. Normally they will have spent several months ahead of the office opening traveling there to build relationships and understand the market. On the other hand, if we have hired someone from outside, they will already know about the market, but they will need to learn about WM's specific needs and requirements and our culture.

When opening new offices, we start with a team of two to three people and quickly acquire a space in a coworking facility. This allows us to stay agile and move swiftly. Once we're ready, we will move to a more permanent leased space that fits our specific needs. Every office must prove its value before moving to a permanent location. Many of our offices begin in coworking spaces and then gradually progress to larger spaces as their teams expand. Ware Malcomb leaders have a saying: you have to earn your way to a long-term location and offices.

Sometimes, we initially rent space from local consultants such as engineering firms. We will use a few desks or occupy a small area, which works well for us, and WM continues to follow this practice on occasion.

Ware Malcomb has created various office structures that cater to different stages of office development, be it a start-up, a small or medium-sized office, or a large office. We have established prototype steps for each stage, which enables offices to observe another one of our offices that is one step ahead of them in growth and learn from it. For example, if an office in Nashville aspires to resemble an established office in Atlanta, they can refer to the prototype steps established for that stage. This approach has been successful for us and saves us from reinventing the wheel every time we initiate a new office.

> **We have established prototype steps for each stage, which enables offices to observe another one of our offices that is one step ahead of them in growth and learn from it. For example, if an office in Nashville aspires to resemble an established office in Atlanta, they can refer to the prototype steps established for that stage.**

As for the pitfalls we face, the most typical one is that it takes longer than planned to break into our targeted market share. We might initially go in with one or two clients, but we have learned to be patient and persistent. It can take some time to establish relationships and trust when entering a new city. Despite being a big firm, since we lack local experience, we need to perform well on projects to gain the trust of current and prospective clients. One may face several obstacles, such as difficulties in closing deals, hiring incompatible staff, market fluctuations, or encountering bumps during a project.

At times, we may not have hired the right leader, and we need to change and start again, which can be challenging. Usually, it's no one's fault, it just didn't work out. It is quite crucial that a leader from outside our firm be a cultural and team fit.

The Acquisition Growth Layer

Acquiring companies can be a risky way to enter new markets, but it can also be rewarding.

For Ware Malcomb, acquisitions are not a primary growth strategy, but we are proud of our approach. We focus on a few key factors when looking for a company to acquire.

First, we are looking for a company that operates in a similar way to us, does the type of work we do, and excels at CRE projects.

Second, we consider whether the company is open to acquisition and whether it could be an excellent cultural fit. Last, we need to determine if the company is adaptable to our way of working, as every company is different.

Ultimately, the cultural fit is the most crucial factor in any acquisition. We need to ensure that the company shares our values and is willing to work with us in a way that benefits both parties. It's always a risk when acquiring another company, but we believe it can be a good strategy if done correctly.

Many times, either the small business owners or their employees struggle to adapt to working for a big company and the culture change that comes with it. This was the case for our first two acquisitions in Chicago and Toronto. However, we strategically chose these markets because our clients were asking us to go there, and they were both big industrial markets that checked all the boxes. In each case, we didn't have an internal leader ready to lead a new office and take part in the Chessboard, which is why we decided to attempt an acquisition. Even though we had never done an acquisition before, we went ahead with them and made a good deal with each one.

Admittedly, the process was a little bumpy, and we faced some challenges. Unfortunately, the leaders who sold us the companies did not remain, and most of the staff eventually departed. However, these acquisitions allowed us to establish market share and recognition, which in turn made them great markets for our company. We learned a lot from those first two acquisitions, and subsequent ones were much smoother, although not without their own challenges. It's important to go into these situations with your eyes open.

Key lesson: if team members from the acquired firm can't fit into your culture, it's okay to make a change.

Acquiring a company and creating a deal that benefits everyone involved can be challenging. However, the *real effort* starts after the deal is closed. This involves hard work to help the acquired company adapt to WM's culture. Also, we need to learn about the market and help people adjust to the changes. These tasks require a lot of attention and effort, especially in a company like ours, where we strive to work as One Team.

Most of our business operations are conducted internally, and we do not rely heavily on consultants. Our CEO, president, CFO, or regional vice president is usually involved in the mergers and acquisitions process within our company. After the deal is completed, all departments, including HR, IT, marketing, production support, and design support, work together closely to ensure a smooth integration with the acquired company. We take pride in our successful track record of acquisitions over the long term, although the first two were challenging in the short term.

Expansion Is a Point of View

Strategy execution in the spirit of the Hedgehog is the foundation of successful market expansion and acquisition. Howard Schultz of Starbucks observed at one of the company's low points that expansion can become an end in itself, an addictive rush. Expansion isn't a strategy, he said; it is a tactic as part of a growth strategy.[34] Keeping that in mind, having a spirit of possibility for your business is the true animating force. Be open to new opportunities and understand that things can change over time. As I said earlier in the book, there's always room for growth, but it doesn't happen automatically.

Though WM didn't initially plan to include Columbus or Nashville in its strategy, these markets have become significant. WM established a presence in both cities, which has been a great success for us. While we have always had many strategic markets on our map, we still haven't established an office in some of them. This is mostly due to timing and other priorities, but we plan to eventually establish offices in those markets. For instance, Boston is a strong market with many different services, and we already have people and a WM footprint there (we have several of these), but we haven't established an office yet. Being flexible and open to new opportunities is essential.

For example, we had an office in Panama for many years, even though it wasn't part of our original strategic plan. However, a long-term opportunity with a particular client made it worthwhile. Eventually, we closed the office since it wasn't a large commercial real estate market, but we still maintain a WM footprint there. Our approach is to target opportunities that have long-term potential and establish offices accordingly.

We have been doing business in Mexico City for many years, and it has been a great experience for us. We have two offices in Mexico, one in Mexico City and another one in Monterrey. Before establishing our offices in Mexico, we used to work for clients who wanted to leverage our design abilities in Mexico, mostly out of our San Diego office.

Over time, we developed expertise in understanding the Mexican economy, government regulations, public affairs, financing, rates of exchange, supply chain, construction methods, and other related issues. Andres Galvis, our principal, who previously ran the Panama office, established our Mexico City office and transferred there to lead the team. He hired an amazing team of local professionals who understand the local customs, the way of working with government agencies, and contractors. Our Mexico City office is one of our most important, and we are grateful for the incredible people working there.

In presentations I've made over the years and countless conversations, I've urged us not to put ourselves in a box defined by self-imposed limitations, those beliefs we accept because society, our industry, or authority figures say they are so.

> In presentations I've made over the years and countless conversations, I've urged us not to put ourselves in a box defined by self-imposed limitations, those beliefs we accept because society, our industry, or authority figures say they are so.

"I am large, I contain multitudes," Walt Whitman wrote in his poem "Song of Myself," and so do our endeavors and enterprises. Amazon started its growth in Jeff Bezos's garage and as a table at publishing conferences. Airbnb was founded in 2008 by Brian Chesky, Joe Gebbia, and Nathan Blecharczyk. To make some extra money, they rented out air mattresses in their apartment during a high-demand event in San Francisco (hence the name). They created a simple website, and in August 2008, the first guests arrived, marking the unofficial launch of Air Bed & Breakfast. Philip Chiang, son of legendary restaurateur Cecilia Sun Yun Chiang, with Paul Fleming, began P.F. Chang's with four small restaurants in Scottsdale, Arizona. Now, the chain has made upscale, high-quality Chinese cooking a Main Street experience at 300 locations worldwide and launched numerous ventures and brands.

Thanks to hundreds of colleagues and allies, Ware Malcomb broke through many of our old expectations. You can do the same.

Bring focus and patience to expansion. Discuss with your clients, friends, and associates. Build a research plan. Start your expansion map today.

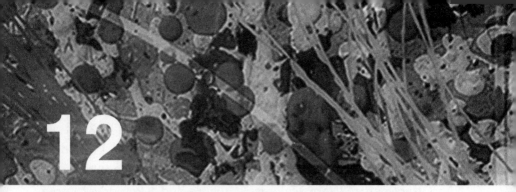

Succession, Posterity, Prosperity: The Final Layers

"The measure of a man is what he does with power."

—Plato

Succession planning is a crucial skill in the development of a leader, especially when it comes to transitioning an office or a company. It is also critical to maintain purposeful growth—to keep the Flywheel turning. Many people struggle with this aspect of their career and business lives, resulting in lost value for all involved.

Delegation and succession planning can be complex and challenging. To avoid confusion, delays, or disagreements, it is essential to have a clear plan in place and work toward it well in advance. Delegation is a crucial part of succession planning and serves as a model for change. It's a learned skill that requires dedication and effort to achieve success.

When Bill and Bill were ready to retire and hand over their firm, they did not want to sell it and have it become a part of another company. They wanted Ware Malcomb to retain its culture and identity under leaders they had trained. This created an incredible opportunity for Jim and me to take over.

It's a theme of this book, my career, and my vision of leadership that when given this kind of opportunity by those who came before you, you have a responsibility to continue this vision and set out to create as many opportunities for people as possible. From designating a Number Two to retirement, succession planning is an important part of Ware Malcomb's culture and a key driver in our leadership academy and other initiatives. It was obvious to me I needed to plan and prepare for succession well in advance, working with trusted advisors and the consultation of the board. When the time came, we wanted to turn the company over to new leaders whom we had trust and confidence in.

> **From designating a Number Two to retirement, succession planning is an important part of Ware Malcomb's culture and a key driver in our leadership academy and other initiatives. It was obvious to me I needed to plan and prepare for succession well in advance, working with trusted advisors and the consultation of the board.**

Why Succession Planning Matters and Why It's Harder Than You Think

Good research by eminent scholars and analysts offers many good answers for the statement above. In my view, human nature explains a lot. Planning for business or life after you're gone isn't appealing to who we are as a species, and particularly if you have a great leadership position. It's good to be king, as the saying goes.

Most of us consider writing a will, final directives, or doing estate planning to be an unpleasant task, not a topic we see hyped on

Facebook or Instagram. "So excited to have finished writing and notarizing my will. Loved making the huge bequest to the pet shelter (sorry, kids)! Thanks to my great lawyer as we celebrate!" posted no one, ever.

The novelist John Sandford observed through one of his characters that the nature of political corruption lies in one irrefutable fact. Being a member of Congress or a US sen-

Rune 2.2 (24" x 24"). Acrylic on canvas.

ator is a powerful, satisfying, and wonderfully head-spinning job you can have, and no one really wants to leave, ever. Succession struggles have been the themes of gripping dramas from *Julius Caesar* to the HBO series of recent fame.

It is not easy to give up the fruits of the tree of leadership. But it is necessary.

"The Holy Grail of Effective Leadership—Succession Planning," an article by Deloitte analysts Jeff Rosenthal, Kris Routch, Kelly Monahan, and Meghan Doherty,[35] argues that succession planning is all about preparing your organization for the future by identifying and developing talented individuals who can step into key roles when needed. It's not just about having a backup plan for when someone leaves but also about building a diverse and strong leadership pipeline that can make better decisions and contribute to a positive organizational culture. It's what we do at Ware Malcomb, and I was determined to carry out my mission to this end.

The analysts point out why organizations struggle with this crucible of leadership. It comes down to the human factor:

> Our study concluded that most companies doing succession planning are often derailed by a host of symptoms that point back to a common culprit—the failure to recognize and address the impact of human behavior on the succession planning process. We found few organizations that were combining a disciplined, data-driven process with a user-friendly, people-centric approach that adequately engages stakeholders. More often than not, we found that companies were either avoiding succession planning altogether or were taking a dispassionate, process-oriented approach that minimizes, or even ignores, the very real impact that it has on the people involved.

Careful, thorough success planning delivers a range of benefits, the authors discovered in their interviews, including:

- A more diverse portfolio of leaders and thought leadership,
- Higher quality decisions about promotions and developmental investments,
- Enhanced career development opportunities for emerging leaders,
- A stronger organizational culture,
- A future-proofed workforce, and
- Greater organizational stability and resilience.[36]

The costs associated with poorly managed CEO and C-suite transitions in the S&P 1500 amount to close to $1 trillion annually, found a 2021 feature article published in *Harvard Business Review*.[37] The well-documented article finds better succession planning would add a full point to the 4–5% annual gains projected for the large cap US equity market, resulting in 20–25% higher company valuations and investor returns. The excessive tendency of large companies to hire leaders from outside is identified as one of the biggest problems with succession practices, causing three major kinds of costs: underperformance, loss of intellectual capital, and lower performance of ill-prepared successors.

I agree that the benefits of internal succession are underappreciated and poorly understood. At Ware Malcomb, leadership means preparing for succession, and although this may not align with every company's approach, our approach has proven benefits.

Hit by a Bus

Emergencies, accidents, health issues, or other external crises pose a more urgent and important challenge to succession planning. Years ago, I'd been thinking about this and had an idea for one of our leadership meetings.

I always start our meetings with a brief discussion about the company or whatever is on my mind. So, this early Thursday morning, as I walked into the meeting, I looked out and posed a hypothetical scenario to my colleagues. I asked them, "I just got hit by a bus. What happens now?"

Then I walked out of the room. I gave them 10 minutes to come up with the answer.

I actually gave them 20 minutes, hanging out in the hallway outside the conference center. Then I returned and was proud that they had come up with a good plan. At the time, Jay was still in the

Chicago office. The leaders in the room decided that Ken and Jay would take over leadership of the company. Jay would immediately move back to Irvine, while they would promote Jay's Number Two to take over the Chicago office. They had a rough outline of the plan to promote others to take over their existing duties and a plan to reach out to all team members, clients, consultants, and industry partners. They also had a plan to execute the life insurance policies we have in place to purchase my stock from my estate. It was a great exercise because it got us thinking about the idea of succession and what happens in such situations. We've referred to this many times over the years since we explored that impromptu exercise.

Having a smooth and orderly succession plan is important, but it becomes even more critical during an emergency situation. It was a good experience for everyone involved. It also provided Tobin, Matt, and other team members with the opportunity to showcase their leadership skills and take charge before we even began thinking about my actual succession plan.

Execute the Plan, as You've Done Many Times

So far, most fortunately, no such eventualities have occurred!

I made the decision to step down as CEO while I still had the energy and drive to keep going. I loved the job in every way. But it's important for a company to avoid stagnation, which is why I didn't want to hold on to my leadership position for too long. In our industry, I've seen many business leaders make the mistake of holding on for too long and not making the necessary arrangements for a smooth transition. To avoid this scenario, I decided to transition and become the chairman instead. This way, I continue to offer my help and guidance to the company while allowing new leaders to take charge, build the company according to their vision, and ensure a controlled and successful exit strategy.

The gist of the plan is that we agreed on a timeline for my chairmanship where I phase back my commitment over time until I ride off into the sunset or, more preferably, the ski slopes and trout streams of Utah. Until then, I'm happily available to assist others, gradually reducing my availability each year. However, there will come a day when I will no longer have that role. That is part of the plan, and it will be all right.

I've had to learn to control my urge to make decisions and be in control through my other pursuits, such as the Orange County United Way campaign to end homelessness. I have a lot to say about these issues and have helped build programs in Orange County. I've freed up time to pursue my art career and serve on the board of the Kent State Foundation. This philosophical approach allows me to avoid burnout and ensure that I am still available to leadership.

Serving as chairman doesn't give me the license to micromanage or interfere. I've made many mistakes, and others will have to make theirs. I've learned that you have to force yourself to let go. It's a bit like raising a child; you can't prevent them from making mistakes.

Developing a strategy for succession planning is as important as developing one for any other aspect of your business. It is crucial to have a plan in place and communicate that plan far ahead of time to the board, and over time to shareholders, all team members, allies, associates, and clients.

Indecisiveness in succession planning can lead to a lot of problems, and it is always better to be prepared than to be caught off guard. In my case, we created a buyout agreement that began three years before my transition, which clearly defined the roles and responsibilities of everyone involved in the process. Although the timing of the transition was not fixed at the time of the agreement, I announced a year ahead of time to the board that the next year would be my last as the CEO. During this period, we gradually delegated more responsibility to other leaders to prepare them for the transition.

> **Indecisiveness in succession planning can lead to a lot of problems, and it is always better to be prepared than to be caught off guard.**

We had a well-planned communications strategy in place. We started by announcing the news internally to our leadership team during end-of-year meetings. At our company holiday party, which had around 1,000 attendees, I announced the news onstage and spoke about our company's progress over the past year, and, of course, offered a long list of thank-yous to Bill and Bill, the team, and our new leaders Ken and Jay. Afterward, we talked to some clients individually, and our team spread the word in the industry. We also released a press statement and used social media to spread the news. It was a great moment for me when I announced it, and it felt like a huge weight had been lifted off my shoulders. It was very freeing.

If You Don't Start, You'll Never Finish

We began planning this transition when I was 57 years old. My buyout began at 60 years old, and I transitioned from CEO to chairman at 63. We'll be done when I'm 70. At the beginning of this process, I had a strong belief that if we didn't start, we would never finish. So we had to start somewhere. I have seen people put together a plan but then become afraid to execute it. This is a common occurrence, even if someone is determined to sell. As the person leaving, you need to have confidence that you will get paid, especially if you are selling internally. You have relinquished control of your business, and you must trust that the people you have turned it over to will do a good job and get you paid. We did not take on any debt to complete this transition.

Some people sell their company to an outside firm or opt for an ESOP (Employee Stock Ownership Plan; a legal structure by which a company's capital stock is bought by its employees or workers) to get their money up front. The issue with an ESOP is that it puts the company in debt, which goes against Ware Malcomb's philosophy. The company has never taken any significant loans, and I certainly didn't want to burden the company with debt. Running the company without any debt has been great for Ware Malcomb in the long term.

It's awesome to have any good strategy in place, but it's equally important to execute on it. Succession is one such strategy. Execution is key to success.

Succession is critical for everything that makes your company what it is. In order to ensure the success of your company, you must be willing to put in the hard work required to find the best people for the correct roles in the firm and then relinquish control. Additionally, the culture of the company is of utmost importance. New leaders can bring fresh ideas and perspectives, which is great, as we should always strive to improve ourselves. However, the foundation and philosophy that led to the success of the company should remain unchanged. We can innovate and evolve while still maintaining our core values.

> **New leaders can bring fresh ideas and perspectives, which is great, as we should always strive to improve ourselves. However, the foundation and philosophy that led to the success of the company should remain unchanged. We can innovate and evolve while still maintaining our core values.**

The Art of Delegation and a Checklist

A well-coordinated, timed succession plan is another form of delegation, which is often misunderstood. It is a skill and an art that requires a lot of effort, especially in the context of mentoring and bringing others along. When done well, delegation is one of the most sophisticated expressions of leadership. We've discussed why this is so earlier in the book.

Turning over your job or a business requires striking a delicate balance. Succession can be threatening for team members who wonder if their jobs are at risk or responsibilities will be changed. Accountability, transparency, communication, and trust are guideposts in formulating a strategy. I recommend that a succession plan include these elements:

- Establish a working group who will meet regularly, most likely members of the board and those you've chosen as successors.

- Establish an atmosphere of openness and trust so all participants feel comfortable asking questions and showing concerns.

- Develop contingency plans for sudden leadership changes or emergencies to ensure the organization can respond effectively to unexpected situations.

- Identify high-potential and high-performing team members and their potential career paths.

- Identify and appoint a new CEO and any other senior officers, and plan for a six-month to one-year consultation and onboarding process.

- Involve your lawyer and accountant to advise you.

- Work with advisors and the board to write up key responsibilities, milestones, and accountabilities for the CEO and other senior officers; engage managers through the ranks to set new goals for growth.

- The financial terms and timelines of the deal will vary from company to company. Include contingencies for different economic and business conditions that may arise during the buyout and transition.

- Develop a thorough, well-planned communications plan.

- Develop a call list of major clients and contact them personally.

These suggestions are prompts for the necessary research and outside consultations appropriate for your situation and station.

Above all, start the process, or you may never finish it.

Florentine Light

In late October, I was honored to travel to Florence for a solo show of my art at Galleria360 located in a beautiful historic district a block from the Arno River. I was thinking a lot about the book on that trip, inspired by the many layers of inspiration we encountered.

I have been working with the Galleria and director Angela Fagu for years, but this time Angela invited me to mount a solo exhibition, and I was joined by Sandy, of course, and close friends from Kent State University. We were all visiting Florence together to celebrate the 50th anniversary of KSU's Study Abroad program.

Layered Vision Solo Show, Galleria360, Florence, Italy.

We gathered for an evening reception, and I could not have been more grateful for the support and work of so many fantastic leaders and designers who made Ware Malcomb the success it is, an international design institution, providing so many opportunities to me such as pursuing this book, taking a deeper dive into my art, and my involvement with Kent State. This Midwest child of the 1960s and hippie college student so inspired and moved by Florence in his early 20s now had the amazing moment of showing my work here with family and friends.

> We gathered for an evening reception, and I could not have been more grateful for the support and work of so many fantastic leaders and designers who made Ware Malcomb the success it is, an international design institution, providing so many opportunities to me such as pursuing this book, taking a deeper dive into my art, and my involvement with Kent State.

I thought about what truly mattered at this moment, as it was time to share my thoughts with our guests. A few excerpts:

> Thank you, Angela. I feel honored to display my work in your studio. Angela and I have been working together for many years, ever since she found me online. I have showcased my art in her gallery many times, and it has been a great working relationship. I am grateful for the opportunity to have a solo show here tonight. Thank you all for coming, especially my friends from Kent State. I appreciate Val [Valoree Vargo, CEO, Kent State Foundation] and her team for helping to organize this event.
>
> Let me tell you a little about my art. I see the world in layers: physical spaces, built and unbuilt work, natural work, and more. My art is an exploration of these layers and how they interact with each other. For example, in this room, there are layers of physical space, sound, and emotion. Each one of us brings layers of our own thoughts and feelings to this space. I try to express this concept in my art.
>
> This particular series is based on the runes of the Proto-Indo-European language and its words for colors. The aim is to express the ancient language in a rough, abstract manner. I

study runes extensively, and I used a roughboard to create this series. The reason for not refining it too much is that I want it to have a rough, ancient look.

And so that's kind of where these come from different moods and emotions as I'm creating them. The two artworks in the window are part of my "FLRs series." They are inspired by my studio floor and created using mixed media. The process involves a digital photograph, overlaid with digital color, then overlaid with acrylic paint. Occasionally, I embed a personal artifact within the artwork. Finally, I add layers of resin to give it a glossy finish. All of these elements come together to create a piece inspired by vignettes on my studio floor. This is an idea that I will continue to explore.

I want to discuss something important with you. My good friend and literary advisor, Cathy Hemming (an icon in the publishing world, a longtime KSU Foundation board member, and a good friend), is assisting me in writing a book on leadership. The book is based on the layers of my company and the various types of input that helped me build it. These inputs range from the influence of Leonardo da Vinci and Vince Lombardi to concepts learned in high school physics class, such as the Visible Light Spectrum, and many other ideas that I have synthesized over time. Cathy has been guiding me throughout the writing process—I have a ghostwriter, and I have a publisher, which is very exciting. We are already halfway through writing the book, and in about a year, you might see it published under the title *Layered Leadership*.

I want to express my gratitude for joining me on this journey. I decided to write this book because I believe the concepts I have described can help people. I'm not a self-proclaimed expert, but I want to share what I've learned with others. I believe growth is crucial, both for individuals and companies, and it is the driving force behind Ware Malcomb, the company that I have dedicated most of my life to. We strive to serve our clients, and we also serve our employees by providing them with opportunities to advance their careers. We have established a leadership academy, and we will continue to do so, even after my tenure on the board is over. I am always available to mentor anyone in need. I hope that this book will act as a guide for anyone interested in synthesizing different concepts to create a thriving organization. You may have your own concepts that you are inspired by, or some of the concepts described here may resonate with you. It's the synthesis of ideas, creativity in implementation, and commitment to execution that will make you successful. My goals will continue to be defined by the opportunities we create for people to develop and excel.

ACKNOWLEDGMENTS

I've thought many times about writing a book, but I never fully committed to it until a conversation came up at a Sunday brunch with our daughter, Lauren Armstrong, PsyD. Lauren encouraged me to write this book, and provided me with the inspiration to follow through on it.

I am very lucky to have a good friend and colleague from our many years serving together on the Kent State University Foundation Board, the great publishing icon Cathy Hemming. Cathy has guided and encouraged me through all of the nuances of the publishing world, and introduced me to my awesome ghostwriter, Herb Schaffner.

Herb helped me organize the structure of this book, helped frame many references and examples of the many woven concepts presented, and expertly translated my words to a cohesive written form.

Bill Ware and Bill Malcomb hired me, guided and mentored me, and gave me so many opportunities, most of all to lead our great company.

Jim Williams was a great partner who taught me so much and provided amazing creative ideas to the growth of our firm.

Members of the WM Board. Each of them powers our firm, provides great leadership, and sets the example for great strategy, execution, and teamwork every day. CEO Ken Wink, President Jay

Todisco, EVP Matt Brady, EVP/CFO Tobin Sloane, VP Operations Radwan Madani, VP of Design Jinger Tapia.

Members of our executive team, Ruth Brajevich, VP, Strategic Initiatives (who provided historical editing); Ted Heisler, VP, Interior Architecture and Design; RVP's Cameron Trefry, Frank DiRoma, Jason Dooley, Tom Jansen, Kevin Evernham; Chris Strawn, VP, Civil Engineering.

Also thanks to additional WM contributors to this book, Maureen Bissonnette, Principal, Marketing; and Ilyes Nouizi, Principal, Resource Services.

My incredible assistant, Monica Birakos, who keeps me organized and provided so much creative work helping with the design of this book, graphics, and layout, as well as coordinating with our in-house and publishing teams.

The WM marketing, graphics, and social media teams, Maria Rodgers, Brandon Cruz, Caitlin Worrell, Noah Burrows.

Current and past WM Team members, who all contributed to WM's success.

Special advisors to the firm, who provide invaluable insight and counsel, Michael Murtaugh and David Hirsch.

Also Ken Kubota, who helped me tremendously early on.

My great friend and marketing genius, Sinan Kanatsiz, and his entire team at KCOMM.

Matt Holt and his amazing team at BenBella Books, for believing in this book and guiding me through the process.

Kent State University, for the incredible education and opportunities, and for the life-changing semester in Florence. To all of my professors, the great CAED Class of 1980, my friends and colleagues on the foundation board, and executives at the university, who have brought so much inspiration.

The MMC. Dave D'Altorio, David Chandler, Scott Warner. Awesome friends, ski and golf partners, who are patient with my slowly developing fly-fishing skills.

Our son, James, whose creativity is boundless.

My father, Robert Armstrong, who was my role model and hero, and taught me everything.

My mother, Phyllis, who helped me find my way, and helped me with my paper route.

My grandmother, Elsie Klenk, who taught me optimism and perseverance.

Most of all, thank you to my beautiful, insightful, creative, funny, supportive, encouraging wife, Sandy.

Nothing in my life happens without her next to me.

This book is a result of every person and influence mentioned, and many unmentioned.

Thank you all.

NOTES

1. Christopher Alexander, *The Nature of Order: An Essay on the Art of Building and the Nature of the Universe, Book 1—The Phenomenon of Life* (Center for Environmental Structure, Vol. 9) 9780972652919: Amazon.com: Books, n.d., https://www.amazon.com/NatureOrderPhenomenonEnvironmental Structure/dp/0972652914.
2. Tim Sablik, "Recession of 1981–82," n.d., Federal Reserve History, https://www.federalreservehistory.org/essays/recession-of-1981-82.
3. Sablik, "Recession of 1981–82."
4. "Top 100 Industrial Sector Architecture Firms for 2023," *Building Design + Construction*, October 11, 2023, https://www.bdcnetwork.com/top-100-industrial-sector-architecture-firms-2023.
5. All credit to the brilliant work of this book: W. Chan Kim and Renée A. Mauborgne, *Blue Ocean Strategy* (Brighton, MA: Harvard Business Review Press, 2005).
6. "Principles Underlying the Drucker Institute's Company Rankings," The Drucker Institute, Claremont Graduate University, n.d., https://drucker.institute/principles-underlying-the-drucker-institutes-company-rankings/.
7. Walter Isaacson, *Leonardo Da Vinci* (New York: Simon and Schuster, 2017).
8. *Nova*, PBS, "Decoding DaVinci," https://www.pbs.org/wgbh/nova/article/leonardodavincianatomydissection/.
9. Original resource extent: 38 pages: ink on paper; 21.3 x 15.3 centimeters. Reference extracted from World Digital Library: Augusto Marinoni, Il Codice del Volo degli uccelli, nella Biblioteca reale di Torino (Florence: GiuntiBarbera, 1976). Peter Jakab, "An Extraordinary Journey: The History of Leonardo da Vinci's Codex on the Flight of Birds," Smithsonian National Air and Space Museum (Washington, DC: September 13, 2013). Original resource at: Royal Library of Turin.
10. "Did Leonardo da Vinci Discover the Ultimate Functional Fitness Training Program?" MidStrong (blog), May 31, 2023, https://www.midstrong.com/resources/leonardo-da-vincis-functional-fitness-training-program.
11. "Leonardo Da Vinci: The Mechanics of Man," n.d., https://www.rct.uk/collection/themes/publications/leonardodavincithemechanicsofman.

12. Martin Kemp, *Leonardo Seen from the Inside Out* (Oxford: Oxford University Press, 2011).
13. Kemp, *Leonardo Seen from the Inside Out.*
14. Gustavo Deco, Martin Kemp, and Morten L. Kringelbach, "Leonardo da Vinci and the Search for Order in Neuroscience," *Current Biology* 31, no. 11 (2021): R704–9, doi:10.1016/j.cub.2021.03.098.
15. Deco, Kemp, and Kringelbach, "Leonardo da Vinci and the Search for Order in Nueroscience."
16. Jeremy Utley, "5 Ways to Boost Creativity on Your Team," *Harvard Business Review*, March 28, 2023, https://hbr.org/2023/03/5waystoboost creativityonyourteam.
17. Robert Lloyd and Wayne Aho, "The Four Functions of Management: An Essential Guide to Management Principles," *Management Open Educational Resources* 1 (2020), doi:10.58809/CNFS7851.
18. Joseph Michelli, "5 Things You Should Not Do in the Name of Customer Experience," The Michelli Experience (blog), May 15, 2018, https://www .josephmichelli.com/blog/should-not-customer-experience/.
19. Claudio Fernández-Aráoz, "Jack Welch's Approach to Leadership," *Harvard Business Review*, March 3, 2020, https://hbr.org/2020/03/jack-welchs -approach-to-leadership.
20. Anjali Shaikh and Kristi Lamar, "Cracking the Code: How CIOs Are Redefining Mentorship to Advance Diversity and Inclusion," Deloitte (blog), March 7, 2019, https://www.deloitte.com/global/en/our-thinking/insights /topics/leadership/cio-insider-business-insights/redefining-mentorship -sponsorship-diversity-inclusion.html.
21. "Mentoring: Why Everyone Benefits from It / Why Everyone Wins with It," Deloitte (blog), August 14, 2018, https://www2.deloitte.com/xe/en/blog /diversity-inclusion/2022/mentoring-why-everyone-benefits-from-it-why -everyone-wins-with-it.html.
22. "Balancing Your Life at Work and Home," *Journal of Oncology Practice* 5, no. 5 (2009): 253255, doi:10.1200/JOP.091018.
23. Leslie Earnest, "HomeBase to Close Stores, Shift Focus," *Los Angeles Times*, December 6, 2000, https://www.latimes.com/archives/la-xpm-2000 -dec-06-fi-61730-story.html.
24. "The Coca-Cola System," The Coca-Cola Company, n.d., https://www.coca -colacompany.com/about-us/coca-cola-system.
25. Leslie McCasker, "What Is Habitat?" Loudoun Wildlife Conservancy, October 1, 2000, https://loudounwildlife.org/2000/10/what-is-habitat/.
26. David Rock and Heidi Grant, "Why Diverse Teams Are Smarter," *Harvard Business Review*, March 19, 2019, https://hbr.org/2016/11/whydiverseteams aresmarter.
27. Donna Kato, "Home Depot Revamps in Tough Economy," *Mercury News*, April 11, 2009, https://www.mercurynews.com/2009/04/11/homedepotrevamps intougheconomy/.
28. Helen Keller, *Helen Keller's Journal: 1936–1937* (New York: Doubleday Doran & Co., 1938), 60.
29. David Guy Powers, *How to Say a Few Words* (New York: Doubleday, 1953).

30. Gina Acosta, "'We're Still Whole Foods': Life After Amazon," *Progressive Grocer*, September 9, 2021, https://progressivegrocer.com/were-still-whole-foods-life-after-amazon.

31. James E. Schrager, "Three Strategy Lessons from GE's Decline," *Chicago Booth Review*, August 14, 2019, https://www.chicagobooth.edu/review/three-strategy-lessons-ge-s-decline.

32. Gary Wolf, "Steve Jobs: The Next Insanely Great Thing," *Wired*, February 1, 1996, https://www.wired.com/1996/02/jobs-2/.

33. "Jim Collins Concepts: The Hedgehog Concept," n.d., https://www.jimcollins.com/concepts/thehedgehogconcept.html.

34. Allen Webb, "Starbucks' Quest for Healthy Growth: An Interview with Howard Schultz," *McKinsey Quarterly*, March 1, 2011, https://www.mckinsey.com/featured-insights/employment-and-growth/starbucks-quest-for-healthy-growth-an-interview-with-howard-schultz.

35. Jeff Rosenthal, Kris Routch, Kelly Monahan, and Meghan Doherty, "The Holy Grail of Effective Leadership Succession Planning," Deloitte Insights, n.d., https://www2.deloitte.com/us/en/insights/topics/leadership/effective leadership succession planning.html.

36. Rosenthal, Routch, Monahan, and Doherty, "The Holy Grail of Effective Leadership Succession Planning."

37. Claudio Fernández Aráoz, "The High Cost of Poor Succession Planning," *Harvard Business Review*, April 13, 2021, https://hbr.org/2021/05/the-high-cost-of-poor-succession-planning.

ABOUT THE AUTHOR

Lawrence R. Armstrong is an acclaimed author, speaker, and artist, as well as the chairman of Ware Malcomb, a leading international design firm. With a career spanning over four decades, Lawrence has been at the forefront of innovative leadership, guiding Ware Malcomb to national prominence, hallmarked by an unprecedented 40x revenue growth. Among his many business accolades, Lawrence was recognized in the OC50, was named three times to the OC500, and received the Excellence in Entrepreneurship Award by the *Orange County Business Journal.* He is chair and founding member of United to End Homelessness, one of Orange County United Way's key initiatives providing supportive housing and care to those experiencing homelessness.

Lawrence's expertise and thought leadership have made him a sought-after speaker and consultant in business. He is an award-winning contemporary artist, specializing in modern art that infuses his architectural acumen and ingenuity to create captivating works. His unique approach integrates art, architecture, and business principles, providing a holistic framework for effective leadership.

Drawing from all aspects of his life, Lawrence's latest accomplishment, *Layered Leadership*, is a book about creativity, driving double-digit growth, and dominating the competition with innovative strategies and execution.

Lawrence is a licensed architect in 45 US states and three Canadian provinces. He is a member of the National Council of Architectural Registration Boards and a LEED Accredited Professional. He received a bachelor of science in architecture and a bachelor of architecture from Kent State University.